THE FACTS ON WHY YOU CAN BELIEVE THE BIBLE

JOHN ANKERBERG
& JOHN WELDON

HARVEST HOUSE PUBLISHERS

EUGENE, OREGON

Cover by Terry Dugan Design, Minneapolis, Minnesota

The Facts on Why You Can Believe the Bible is adapted with new research from *Knowing the Truth about the Reliability of the Bible, The Facts on False Views of Jesus: The Truth Behind the Jesus Seminar,* and short excerpts from *Ready with an Answer.*

THE FACTS ON SERIES
John Ankerberg and John Weldon
The Facts on Halloween
The Facts on Homosexuality
The Facts on Islam
The Facts on Jehovah's Witnesses
The Facts on Roman Catholicism
The Facts on the King James Only Debate
The Facts on the Masonic Lodge
The Facts on the Mormon Church
The Facts on Why You Can Believe the Bible
The Facts on World Religions

THE FACTS ON WHY YOU CAN BELIEVE THE BIBLE

Copyright © 2004 by John Ankerberg and John Weldon
Published by Harvest House Publishers
Eugene, Oregon 97402
www.harvesthousepublishers.com

Library of Congress Cataloging-in-Publication Data

Ankerberg, John, 1945-
 The facts on why you can believe the Bible / John Ankerberg and John Weldon.
  p. cm.—(Facts on series)
 Includes bibliographical references.
 ISBN 0-7369-1464-1 (pbk.)
 1. Bible—Evidences, authority, etc. I. Weldon, John. II. Title. II. Series.
 BS480.A68 2004
 220.1—dc22   2004006491

Printed in the United States of America

04 05 06 07 08 09 10 / VP-KB / 10 09 08 07 06 05 04 03 02 01

CONTENTS

Section I
The Bible and the Difference It Makes

Section II
The Accuracy and Supernatural Character of the Biblical Text

Section III
The Responsibility of Historical Research

SECTION I

The Bible
and the Difference
It Makes

"So many of the ideas that found application in America's founding documents and our government were taken from the Bible. It is not only the single most cited authority in the writings of the founding Era, but it is also the book from which many of America's political and social customs were originally formed." (David Barton, *The Influence of the Bible on America*)

1
Does the Bible matter?

Christian faith is increasingly under assault today, even in America, the nation that has benefited so extraordinarily from its positive influence in national and individual life. Ironically, many are now expressing open disdain for the Christian faith that has provided their freedoms—among them secularists, liberals, humanists, multiculturalists, politicians, and even leaders in religion. Such disdain could be seen as one of the great ironies of recent time. Skeptics and others who wish to tear down the Bible and Christian faith should actually be on their knees thanking God for both, because otherwise they would clearly not have the blessings and freedoms for their personal endeavors. Whatever shortcomings Christian faith has expressed throughout history, they pale in insignificance to the incalculable blessings it has produced for America and throughout the world. And the benefits are due largely to one factor: the teachings of the Bible lived out in practical ways by men and women who believed it. When we examine the benefits of Christian faith to humankind, we must remember it is the Bible that plays the central role.

Because this is a book about trusting the Bible, perhaps the most appropriate place to begin is by briefly illustrating for people how the Bible has dramatically impacted their lives. A number of books and papers have been written on this topic, but those we would recommend most for additional study are by Alvin J. Schmidt, *Under the Influence: How Christianity Transformed Civilization*; D. James Kennedy, *What If Jesus Had Never Been Born?* and *What If the Bible Had Never Been Written?*; and the paper by Professor Paul Johnson, "The Necessity of Christianity."[1]

Put simply, without the influence of the Bible, there wouldn't be an America, let alone a Western civilization where people have the freedom to censure expressions of Christian faith. Christianity deserves credit for many of the great political, social, humanitarian, scientific, educational, and cultural advances in the Western world. The Bible, it seems, has inspired most of the great writers, artists, educators, scientists, politicians, and educators.

Contrarily, those who seek to undermine or destroy Christian influence merely engage in a form of cultural suicide: They destroy the very possibility of building the better life they seek.

Examples of areas where Christianity has exerted a profound and positive influence on Western civilization include:

- the founding and development of modern science and law

- the founding and development of medicine and health care, involving the first establishing of hospitals

- modern education, including the founding of nearly all major American universities, such as Princeton, Harvard, Yale, and Dartmouth

- providing a logical basis through absolute values for the advance of ethics in general, including sexual morality, which in our time alone has saved millions of lives

- protecting the dignity of marriage and family life, which greatly contributes to the stabilization of society

- instituting political freedom and human rights generally, including the abolition of slavery and protection of the unborn, infants, children, and women

- inspiring major contributions to the best in art, literature, music, and architecture

- undergirding vast humanitarian endeavors globally, supporting the dignity of labor and economic reform

And the list goes on and on.

Women, children, slaves, the sick, the unborn, the uneducated, the persecuted, those mentally ill, abandoned, or dying—virtually no category of the vulnerable has been left unembraced by Christian faith. The Red Cross, the Salvation Army, public education (which originated with the Protestant reformers), modern capitalism, property rights and private property, workers' protection, women's human rights, political freedom and democracy, the idea of liberty and justice for all—all owe their support or existence to biblical ideals. The difference between the pre-Christian world and the post-Christian is like night and day, and the Bible made the difference.

Indeed, to cite one example in our modern era, the world itself is safer at present and an entire nation of 300 million people is free today because of one man's Christian faith—because of his personal trust in Christ and his belief in the Bible. President Ronald Reagan almost single-handedly dismantled the Soviet Union because he believed he was called to this task and trusted God for the outcome. He won the Cold War and freed the Soviet Union, reinvigorated America, and so much else because he had believed in Christ from a young age, spent hours on his knees in prayer, and was dominated by his faith—undoubtedly one reason his life was so richly blessed. The incredible, near-insurmountable goal of dismantling a godless Soviet state was borne in part because of his desire to give the Russian people freedom of religion for their very souls' sake. As explained in his famous March 8, 1983, "Evil Empire" speech, he believed that "we're enjoined by Scripture and the Lord Jesus to oppose it with all our might." (See Paul Kengor, *God and Ronald Reagan*, 2004).

All this and more is why those who are Christians should be proud of the Bible, proud to be sure. But those who wish to undermine Christian influence in the world should recognize their liability for taking part in actively destroying so much of what is good in the world. Alas, most of the above advantages are currently in the process of deterioration, largely from the alarming impact of an amoral secularization that wants Christian influence done and gone. One only need witness the recent corrosion of education, law, morality, cultural entertainment (such as TV and music), family life, and even freedom itself. What was once noble and great is increasingly frayed and profane. And again, the more people tear down the Bible and Christian faith, the more they contribute to the very process that will destroy their own future and others'. Of course, what can never be destroyed is the eternal. The practical day-to-day benefits everyone experiences from the Bible pale in comparison to the spiritual benefits Christian faith has conveyed upon untold millions globally, but that is the subject of another book. Here we discuss *the* Book.

In the history of mankind, if even a billion books have been written, only one is extraordinary. Among even the sacred books of the world, none comes close, and one only need read them to appreciate the truth of it. The Bible's influence in history is incalculable: It has literally changed the world; not just Western history, but all of history. Abraham Lincoln called the Bible "the best gift God has given to man," while Immanuel Kant echoed him: "The Bible is the greatest benefit which the human race has ever experienced." Patrick Henry understood: "It is worth all other books which were ever printed," and so did William Gladstone: "An immeasurable distance separates it from all competitors." A.M. Sullivan correctly observed that "the cynic who ignores, ridicules or denies the Bible, spurning its spiritual rewards and aesthetic excitement, contributes to his own moral anemia." Such citations could be multiplied almost endlessly.[2]

No book written has had more influence upon the world. Given the impact, it's rather astonishing that hundreds of millions of people among the most educated nations are fundamentally ignorant of its contents. Imagine that. Since the ideals of education cannot explain it, perhaps only willful unbelief can. As Aldous Huxley once noted: "Most ignorance is vincible ignorance. We don't know because we don't want to know."[3]

It seems that most people prefer not to study the Bible because they intuitively recognize it would interfere with how they wish to live. As a result, the Bible experiences endless assaults on its credibility from academics, professional skeptics, religious and cultural leaders, and so on, which are eventually absorbed by the population in general. Now everyone can relax.

Not surprisingly, in a world of unbelief only a relatively small percentage of people accept the Bible as the literal, inerrant Word of God. Unfortunately, in addition to cultural and emotional bias, another part of the problem can be found in the Christian church itself, which has often failed to adequately educate its members about the Bible, not only doctrinally but evidentially as well. It is unlikely that one will grant support to the content of the Bible unless one is convinced its content is accurate and authoritative.

Not only the general public, but many in the church remain uninformed as to the trustworthiness of the Bible, and it is because of this we have written this booklet. The simple fact is that 2000 years of careful investigation by believers and unbelievers alike have reasonably proven the following assertion: The Bible is the Word of God without demonstrable error—despite its age, authorship, and many critics. In this book we will explain why, and also why its critics lack a leg to stand on. We think it is significant that, given 2000 years of the most intense scrutiny by critics and skeptics, millions of people in the modern era continue to believe the Bible is the literal inerrant Word of God—and argue it can be rationally defended as such. Can members of any other religious faith in the world logically prove such a claim concerning their own scripture?

2

What have been the different approaches to establishing the reliability of the Bible?

Over time there have been a variety of well-reasoned and objective approaches for establishing the reliability of the Bible. Among them are:

- *Its prophetic accuracy*—The Bible's remarkable predictions, which, due to their specific nature, cannot logically be explained apart from divine inspiration.

- *The testimony of Jesus Christ*—His complete endorsement of the Old Testament as the inerrant Word of God and His pre-authentication of the New Testament offer the strongest proof of biblical trustworthiness because of who Christ is. Because Jesus is God incarnate, as proven by His unparalleled life, spectacular miracles, and resurrection from the dead, He stands as an infallible authority, and in that position He taught the Bible was the literal Word of God.

- *The manuscript evidence*—This proves the Bible has not experienced textual corruption, as critics argue, but is virtually autographic.

- *The archaeological data*—The striking fact that over a century of detailed, scientific archaeological excavations have failed to prove a *single* biblical statement incorrect, while confirming as accurate thousands of historical, geographical, and other details in the Bible. This cannot easily be explained apart from divine inspiration, again making the Bible unique among all ancient books ever written.

- *Its amazing scientific prevision*—Scores of biblical statements conform to facts of modern science, even before these facts were known, something inexplicable on naturalistic grounds. As with its prophetic and archaeological accuracy, this can only be explained through divine inspiration.

- *Additional approaches*—The Bible's unique claims, internal unity, recorded miracles, and historic preservation set it apart from all other books and require an explanation for its origin beyond the natural. Indeed, the Bible's overall uniqueness, dramatic power to change lives, and the simple fact it can still rationally be claimed to be the Word of God and logically defended as such—despite 2000 years of intense criticism by the best arguments of the world's leading skeptics—reveal what an amazing book it is.

Far more than a book, it remains mankind's principal treasure.

3

Why is the reliability of the Bible a critical subject for everyone?

Why is the subject of this book, the reliability of the Bible, such a crucial one? It is critical because of its implications. The Bible is the most important book in the world because it alone *is* God's Word. To be ignorant concerning its claims and contents constitutes an abdication of personal responsibility, not to mention public education.

If the Bible *is* the Word of God, then its importance to every person and every culture is obvious. Religious scripture that is simply a human product, false or mythic, can hardly command authority. And this is the lot of all non-biblical scripture, despite what anyone claims, and no matter how unpleasant we are to some for saying it. So, the only question at this point is whether or not there is real evidence to support the Bible's claims to be genuine divine revelation.

If the Bible is the inerrant Word of God, and if it authoritatively answers the fundamental questions of life, then who can logically be passive and ignore its teachings? If the Bible accurately tells us who *God* is, who *we* are, *why* we are here, and what *happens* when we die, is there a living soul anywhere who should fail to be impressed? If the Bible gives us reassuring absolutes in a world of menacing relatives, doesn't this introduce profound implications? Who wants to live a life of insecurity and hopelessness when they can actually know the truth with certainty?

Indeed, isn't the plague of the modern world its own relativism—in ethics, law, politics, sexuality, education, psychotherapy, medicine, religion, business, and so on? If people live only for themselves and do whatever they want—often in disregard of others' welfare—isn't the major reason for this because they feel life is meaningless and that nothing finally matters but their own interests? If there is no final authority in anything, and if when you die you are gone forever, why not live any way you want?

It would be difficult to deny that if people today lived according to most of the Ten Commandments, just a "small" set of laws, that most of our national social ills would be solved or greatly reduced. People don't live that way because they do not really believe those words and commandments came from God. And they certainly don't believe that God will hold them accountable in the next life for the kind of life they lived here.

In essence, helping people to trust the Bible and live by its precepts is the single most important issue for our nation's direction and future. It is the one single item that would solve most of our problems immediately, heal our nation, and prosper us again in every way. If so, then the subject of this booklet must be of great importance.

To know the Bible is reliable is to know that *all* of what it teaches is reliable. And what it teaches is that the one true God sent His only Son to die for our sins so that we could inherit eternal life as a free gift. Such a declaration is unparalleled. If skeptics are given only one reason to examine the claims of the Bible, this should be the paramount one. Because, if true, then it offers more than they could possibly imagine. Conversely, if the Bible is true and one rejects its message of salvation, then no other personal decision will be more consequential. Therefore, no one can logically fail to ignore the issue of the reliability of the Bible.

4

What does the Bible claim for itself, and is there good reason to believe it?

The Bible contains some 1200 promises, 3000 questions, and 6000 commands; some 8000 verses having predictions of the future, and it mentions God some 10,000 times. And in various ways, the Bible consistently claims to be God's Word—absolutely authoritative, inerrant, immutable, truthful, and eternal:

- "All Scripture is inspired by God" (2 Timothy 3:16 NASB).

- "The Scripture cannot be broken" (John 10:35).

- "Thy word is truth" (John 17:17 KJV).

- "Heaven and earth will pass away, but my words will never pass away" (Matthew 24:35).

- "Every word of God is tested" (Proverbs 30:5 NASB).

- "The words of the Lord are pure words, as silver tried in a furnace on the earth, refined seven times" (Psalm 12:6 NASB).

- "For you have been born again not of seed which is perishable but imperishable, that is, through the living and enduring word of God" (1 Peter 1:23 NASB).

- "Forever, O LORD, thy word is settled in heaven" (Psalm 119:89 KJV).

- "For truly I say to you, until heaven and earth pass away, not the smallest letter or stroke shall pass from the Law until all is accomplished" (Matthew 5:18 NASB).

- "But He answered and said, 'It is written, "Man shall not live on bread alone, but on every word that proceeds out of the mouth of God."'" (Matthew 4:4 NASB)

- "But the word of the Lord endures forever" (1 Peter 1:25 NASB).[4]

If the Bible is really the Word of God, an errorless original text is what one would expect from a truthful God. But what a seemingly difficult proposition to defend in a modern scientific world, especially since we don't have the original manuscripts. Indeed, even if we had them, could 40-plus writers from highly divergent backgrounds and temperaments—kings, tax collectors, prophets, physicians, exiles, fishermen—writing over a period of 1500 years from 1450 B.C. to A.D. 50, on scores of different subjects, in widely varying and difficult circumstances, including persecution; writing history in extremely specific detail, even giving hundreds and hundreds of predictions of the future—plus much more that would make errors a certainty—could all of them to the last man have written something the size of the Bible without a single error? At ten hours a day it takes seven days just to read the Bible—if you read fast. Talk about the supernatural. Try generating an errorless text that size with 66 books and 40 authors over 1500 years with any other group of writers in history. Indeed, just try it with any ten books and five writers over 50 years. Yet the evidence strongly suggests the Bible is inerrant, and again, only divine inspiration can account for it.

A good general definition of biblical inerrancy is given by Dr. Paul Feinberg: "Inerrancy means that when all facts are known, the Scriptures in their original autographs and properly interpreted will be shown to be wholly true in everything that they affirm, whether that has to do with doctrine or morality or with the social, physical, or life sciences."[5] There are three principal lines of evidence for the inerrancy of the Bible, properly understood.[6] These involve claim, testimony, and data: 1) the Bible's own claim to be the literal word of God, as illustrated above, is not made from thin air, but is supported by its demonstrated credibility in other areas; 2) the testimony of Jesus, the final authority in whatever He taught, encompasses the most important evidence; and 3) the lack of a single proven error, despite innumerable critical examinations of biblical data by both skeptics and believers for millennia.

5

Did Jesus believe the Bible was without error?

The strength of the case for Jesus' view of inerrancy is seen by a detailed study of His absolute trust in and use of

Scripture as seen, for example, in the detailed, authoritative study of Christ's view of Scripture by John Wenham in *Christ and the Bible*.[7] If it were otherwise, Jesus would positively have told us that there were errors and corrected them, but even this is illogical, for it presumes either errant divine inspiration or a lack of providential preservation of the text. For Jesus, what Scripture said, God said—period. Not once did He say, "This Scripture is in error" and proceed to correct it. The testimony of Jesus Christ to the reliability of the Old Testament is indisputable (e.g., John 17:17). As God (John 5:17-18; 10:30), Jesus Christ is omniscient; in that authoritative role He authenticated the strict, literal, historical accuracy of the Old Testament, including the narratives most often rejected as mythological by the critics, such as Creation, Noah's flood, Jonah and the whale, Daniel, and so on: "It is of the Old Testament without any reservation or exception that he says, it 'cannot be broken.'...He affirms the unbreakableness of the Scripture in its entirety and leaves no room for any such supposition as that of degrees of inspiration and fallibility. Scripture is inviolable. Nothing less than this is the testimony of our Lord. And the crucial nature of such witness is driven home by the fact that it is in answer to the most serious of charges and in the defense of his most stupendous claim that he bears this testimony."[8]

Critical defenses of inerrancy have been successfully argued by Sproul, Montgomery, Feinberg, and others.[9] A logical defense of inerrancy may be constructed based on historical argument centering on Christ's resurrection. Following the arguments of Montgomery and Sproul,[10] a series of points can be given to show how definitively the historical fact of Christ's resurrection proves the inerrancy of the Bible.

First, on the basis of accepted principles of historic and textual analysis, the New Testament documents are shown to be reliable and trustworthy historical documents (see Qs. 3 and 6). Second, in the Gospel records, Jesus claimed to be God incarnate (John 5:18; 10:27-33). But He didn't just claim it like one mentally ill, He proved it like no other person in history. He exercised innumerable divine prerogatives, and He rested His claims on His numerous eyewitnesses and historically unparalleled miracles (John 10:37-38), including His repeatedly prophesied physical resurrection from the dead (John 10:17-18). Third, in each Gospel Christ's resurrection is minutely described, and for 2000 years it has been incapable of disproof despite the detailed scholarship of the world's best skeptics. In sum, the historic fact of Christ's resurrection from the dead proves His claim to deity. Because Jesus is literally God, He is automatically, of necessity, an infallible authority, incapable of speaking error (John 12:48-50; Matthew 24:35). And He clearly taught that Scripture originates from God and is inerrant, since that which originates from an utterly trustworthy, immutable God must be utterly trustworthy and immutable itself. Again, if Jesus is God, what God says is true by definition and therefore His unqualified teaching on the inerrancy of the Scriptures proves the validity of the inerrancy position. In John 17:17, and Matthew 4:4 He could only have referred to the complete Old Testament canon of the Jews then extant (Luke 24:27). No less an authority than Jesus affirmed 100 percent of the Old Testament as inspired and therefore inerrant. (See John 1:1; 5:46; 8:14-16,26,28; 12:48-50; 14:6; 2 Peter 1:20; Philippians 2:1-8; Titus 2:13.)

If you had to bet the farm, would you bet it on the convictions of those with groundless critical assumptions, who have never performed even one miracle, or on those of the only man in history to frequently claim beforehand that He would rise from the dead and actually do it? As theologian, historian, and trial attorney, Dr. John Warwick Montgomery observes, "The weight of Christ's testimony to Scripture is so much more powerful than any alleged contradiction or error in the text or any combination of them, that the latter must be adjusted to the former, not the reverse."[11]

The third evidence for inerrancy is seen in the biblical data itself—that, despite some currently irresolvable problems arising from insufficient information, no error has ever been proven. Again, this is a virtual miracle. And it is simply impossible to account for books like Zephaniah, Obadiah, and Nahum that are over 70 percent predictive apart from an omniscient God who knows the future and has reliably revealed it.

SECTION II

The Accuracy and Supernatural Character of the Biblical Text

6

Why would anyone argue that the Bible can't be trusted?

Otherwise brilliant scientists, average college students and their professors, and skeptics of all stripes argue that the Bible cannot be trusted. However attentive they may be to facts in other areas, in this area they speak largely on the basis of unjustified assumptions, bias, and/or simple ignorance of the facts. To argue against the facts is neither wise nor evidence of education. How do we know that the Bible is accurate and trustworthy in history, religion, science, and whatever else it may speak on? Consider seven points that the factually challenged normally ignore.

Fact One: Manuscript Preservation

The biblical text is *far* more accurately preserved than any other text of ancient history, and to declare otherwise is nonsense. There are far more New Testament manuscripts copied with far greater accuracy and far earlier dating than for *any* secular classic from antiquity. The New Testament has a fragment within about a generation of its original composition, whole books within about 100 years from the time of the originals, most of the New Testament in less than 200 years, and the entire New Testament within 250 years from the date of its completion. Collectively there are thousands of New Testament manuscripts and portions.[12] The Gospels are extremely close to the events which they record. The first three can be dated as early as 20 years or so of the events cited, and this may even be true for the fourth gospel (see Fact 6). Regardless, all four Gospels were written during the lives of eyewitnesses, and abundant opportunity existed for those with contrary evidence to examine the witnesses and refute them.

The Old Testament was also incredibly preserved, and its overall historical accuracy has been factually confirmed, as illustrated in scholarly texts such as K.A. Kitchen's *On the Reliability of the Old Testment* (2003) and Walter C. Kaiser's *The Old Testament Documents: Are*

They Reliable and Relevant? (2001). For example, a detailed comparison of the Qumran and Massoretic Old Testament texts reveal, in the words of Dr. Ron Rhodes, "they are essentially the same, with very few changes," despite more than 1000 years of copying (www.ron rhodes.org/manuscript.html). The fact that manuscripts separated by a thousand years are essentially the same indicates the incredible accuracy of the Old Testament's manuscript transmission. Indeed, if the Bible were simply an assortment of secular writings, no fair-minded scholar in the world would suggest its textual unreliability.

While collectively there are thousands of copies of the individual biblical books, and while each of the manuscript copies differ, as one would expect, the differences are generally minor, not major. For example, Dr. Ron Rhodes supplies the following New Testament illustration:

Manuscript 1: **Jesus** Christ is the Redeemer of the whole **worl**.

Manuscript 2: **Christ** Jesus is the Redeemer of the whole world.

Manuscript 3: Jesus Christ **s** the Redeemer of the whole world.

Manuscript 4: Jesus Christ is **th** Redeemer of the **whle** world.

Manuscript 5: Jesus Christ is the Redeemer of the whole **wrld**.[13]

Reconstructing the original in this sample is easy, as it is generally for the entire New Testament—to an original accuracy of more than 99 percent, with the remaining uncertainties being insignificant.

There are 5300 extant Greek manuscripts and portions, 10,000 Latin Vulgate, and 9300 other versions. The papyri and early uncial manuscripts date much closer to the originals than for any other ancient literature. For example, of 16 well-known classical authors (Plutarch, Tacitus, Suetonius, Polybius, Thucydides, Xenophon, and others), the total number of extant copies is typically *less than ten,* and the earliest copies date from 750 to 1600 years *after* the original manuscript was first penned.[14] We need only compare this slender evidence to the mass of biblical documentation involving over 24,000 manuscript portions, manuscripts, and versions, the earliest fragments and complete copies dating between 50 and 300 years after originally written.

No ancient literature has ever supplied historians and textual critics with such an abundance of data. It is this wealth of material that has enabled scholars such as Westcott and Hort, Ezra Abbott, Philip Schaff, A.T. Robertson, Norman Geisler, and William Nix to place the restoration of the original text at 99 percent plus.[15] Thus, no other document of the ancient period is as accurately preserved as the New Testament: "Hort's estimate of 'substantial variation' for the New Testament is one-tenth of 1 percent; Abbot's estimate is one-fourth of 1 percent; and even Hort's figure including trivial variation is less than 2 percent. Sir Frederic Kenyon well summarizes the situation:

> The number of manuscripts of the New Testament…is so large that it is practically certain that the true reading of every doubtful passage is preserved in some one or another of these ancient authorities. This can be said of no other ancient book in the world.[16]

How can the New Testament possibly be rejected as "unreliable" when its documentation is at least 100 times that of other ancient literature that is widely accepted? Because it is impossible to question the world's ancient classics that the scholarly community accepts largely without question, it is far more impossible to question the Bible. In other words, those who question the reliability of the Bible must also question the reliability of virtually every ancient writing the world possesses! In effect, to throw out the Bible is to throw out ancient history and shut down classics departments everywhere.

Fact Two: Archaeology

Archaeology has repeatedly and dramatically confirmed the accuracy of the biblical narratives in both Testaments. What scholars once considered myth is, time and again, proven sober history. (See Q. 7.)

Fact Three: Incontrovertible Conviction of Truth

No proven fraud or error exists on the part of any New or Old Testament author. Do the writers contradict themselves? Is there anything in their writing which causes one to objectively suspect their trustworthiness? The answer is no. But there is evidence of careful eyewitness reporting throughout the New and Old Testaments. The caution exercised by the writers, their personal conviction that what they wrote was true, and the lack of demonstrable error or contradiction indicate that the authors told the truth (cf., Luke 1:1-4; John 19:35; 21:24; Acts 1:1-3; 2:22; 26:24-26; 2 Peter 1:16; 1 John 1:1-3). As far as the New Testament, e.g., the physician Luke emphasized his personal care in reporting: "I myself have carefully investigated everything from the beginning...so that you may know the certainty of the things you have been taught" (Luke 1:3-4). "After his [Jesus'] suffering, he showed himself to these men [apostles] and gave many convincing proofs that he was alive. He appeared to them over a period of forty days and spoke about the kingdom of God" (Acts 1:3). Luke's careful historical writing has been documented from detailed archaeological data by Sir William Ramsey, who stated after his painstaking investigations, "Luke's history is unsurpassed in respect of its trustworthiness."[17] A.N. Sherwin-White, the distinguished historian of Rome, stated of Luke: "For [the book of] Acts the confirmation of historicity is overwhelming. Any attempt to reject its basic historicity even in matters of detail must now appear absurd.[18] The apostle John likewise emphasized: "This is the disciple who testifies to these things [about Jesus] and who wrote them down. We know that his testimony is true" (John 21:24).

The many powerful enemies of Jesus and the apostolic church would have proven fraud or pointed out other serious problems had they been able to—but the silence is deafening. The complete inability of the numerous adversaries of Jesus and the early Church to discredit Christian claims (when they had both the motive and ability to do so) argues strongly for their veracity.

Fact Four: Sources Outside the New Testament

The church fathers extensively cite the New Testament. There are some 36,000 early (A.D. 100–300) patristic quotations of the New Testament—such that all but a few verses of the entire New Testament could be reconstructed from these alone.[19] The existence of both Jewish and secular accounts, to a significant degree, confirm the picture of Christ we have in the New Testament. For example, scholarly research by Dr. Gary R. Habermas in *Ancient Evidence for the Life of Jesus* and other works indicates that "a broad outline of the life of Jesus" and His death by crucifixion can be reasonably and directly inferred from entirely non-Christian sources.[20]

24

Fact Five: Eyewitnesses

The presence of hundreds of eyewitnesses to the events recorded in the New Testament would surely have prohibited any major distortion of the facts, just as today any false reporting as to the major events of any war would be corrected on the basis of living eyewitnesses and historic records. The Gospel writers could not have gotten away with myth-making, given what was at stake for both Christ's followers and His enemies. They time and again maintained that these things were not done in a corner, that they were literally eyewitnesses of the miraculous events of Jesus' life, and that their testimony should be believed because it was true. And none has ever shown otherwise:

- "We were witnesses of these things" (Acts 5:32).

- "We did not follow cleverly invented stories" (2 Peter 1:16).

- "I stand here and testify to small and great alike. I am saying nothing beyond what the prophets and Moses said would happen…. What I am saying is true and reasonable. The king is familiar with these things, and I can speak freely to him. I am convinced that none of this has escaped his notice, because it was not done in a corner" (Acts 26:22,25-26).

Significantly, unlike any other religious leader, Jesus frequently appealed to His ability to prove His claims to deity by predicting the future or performing spectacular miracles, such as healing those born blind or raising the dead: "I am telling you now before it happens, so that when it does happen you will believe that I am He" (John 13:19). "Believe me when I say that I am in the Father and the Father is in me; or at least believe on the evidence of the miracles themselves" (John 14:11). When Jesus healed the paralytic (Mark 2:8-11), He did so "that you may know that the Son of Man has authority on earth to forgive sins" (verse 10)—for Jews, an obvious claim to being God. In John 10:33 the Jewish leaders accused Jesus of blaspheming because He was claiming to be God. What was Jesus' response? "Do not believe me unless I do what my Father does. But if I do it, even though you do not believe me, believe the miracles, that you may know and understand that the Father is in me, and I in the Father" (John 10:37-38)—another evident claim to deity. Many other examples could be added showing the power of eyewitness testimony to biblical reliability.

Fact Six: Critics and Skeptics

The fact that both conservative scholars (e.g., F.F. Bruce, John Wenham) and liberal scholars (e.g., Bishop A.T. Robinson) have penned defenses of New Testament reliability is a witness to the strength of the data. For example, in *Redating Matthew, Mark and Luke*, noted conservative British scholar John Wenham presents a convincing argument that the synoptic Gospels are to be dated before A.D. 55. He dates Matthew at A.D. 40 (some tradition says the early 30s); Mark at A.D. 45, and Luke no later than A.D. 51–55.[21] And liberal bishop John A.T. Robinson argued in his *Redating the New Testament* that the New Testament was written and in circulation between A.D. 40–65.[22] But it would not surprise us to discover the synoptics were written before A.D. 40, within ten years of the death of Christ.[23]

The implications of an early New Testament are anything but small. A New Testament written before A.D. 70 absolutely destroys the edifice on which higher critical premises regarding the New Testament are based. If true, insufficient time now remains for the early church to have supposedly embellished the records with their own alleged inventions about Jesus. Even the cream of the critical methods themselves indirectly support New Testament reliability with consistent scholarly, factual reversals of their conclusions, undermining *their* credibility, not the Bible's. Although higher critical theories reject biblical reliability by mere supposition, nevertheless, when such theories "are subjected to the same analytical scrutiny as they apply to the New Testament documents, they will be found to make their own contribution to validating the historicity of those records."[24] Even 200 years of scholarly rationalistic biblical criticism (such as form, source, and redaction approaches) have proven nothing except that the writers were careful and honest reporters of the events recorded and that these methods attempting to discredit them are flawed and biased from the start.[25]

And what of the many capable or brilliant skeptics in every generation who have converted to Christianity largely on the basis of the historical evidence—Saul of Tarsus, Athanagoras, Augustine, George Lyttleton and Gilbert West, Cyril Joad, John Warwick Montgomery, C.S. Lewis, Frank Morison, Sir William Ramsay, Malcolm

Muggeridge, Lew Wallace, Lee Strobel, and on and on. For Bible critics to be right, such men must be either naïve or fools.[26] The fact that critics and skeptics have done so poorly over the ages says more than they are willing to concede.

Fact Seven: Legal Evidence

Many additional logical and legal reasons document biblical reliability. For example, critics argue that Jesus Christ was not who the disciples claim He was in the New Testament, but merely an unusual Jewish prophet whom the disciples made into a divine savior. What this means is that to the last man, the disciples all suffered severe persecution and later died for what they *knew* was a lie. If anything is illogical, it's sacrificing your life for what you absolutely know is phony. The disciples gave their lives solely because the evidence convinced them Christ was who He claimed to be; mere subjective "evidence" had nothing to do with it.

Lawyers, of course, are expertly trained in the matter of evaluating evidence and are perhaps the most qualified in the task of weighing data critically. Is it coincidence that so many of the best legal minds throughout history have concluded in favor of the truth of the Christian religion, and on the grounds of strict legal evidence alone accepted the New Testament as factual history?

Consider the "father of international law," Hugo Grotius, who wrote *The Truth of the Christian Religion* (1627) or the single greatest authority on English and American common-law evidence in the nineteenth century, Harvard Law School professor Simon Greenleaf, who wrote *Testimony of the Evangelists*, in which he powerfully demonstrated the reliability of the Gospels.[27] There is also Edmund H. Bennett (1824–1898), who for over 20 years was the Dean of Boston University Law School and penned *The Four Gospels From a Lawyer's Standpoint* (1899).[28] Irwin Linton represented cases before the Supreme Court and wrote *A Lawyer Examines the Bible* (1943, 1977), in which he stated:

> So invariable had been my observation that he who does not accept wholeheartedly the evangelical, conservative belief in Christ and the Scriptures has never read, has forgotten, or never been able to weigh—and certainly is utterly unable to refute—the irresistible force of the cumulative evidence upon which such faith rests, that there seems ample ground, for the conclusion that such ignorance is an invariable element

in such unbelief. And this is so even though the unbe-
liever be a preacher, who is supposed to know this subject if he know no other.[29]

Certainly, such men were well-acquainted with legal
reasoning and have just as certainly concluded that the
evidence for the historic truthfulness of Scripture is
beyond reasonable doubt. As apologist, theologian, and
lawyer, John W. Montgomery observes in *The Law Above
the Law* that the "ancient documents" rule (that ancient
documents constitute competent evidence if there is no
evidence of tampering and they have been accurately
transmitted); the "parol evidence" rule (Scripture must
interpret itself without foreign intervention); the
"hearsay rule" (the demand for primary-source evidence);
and the "cross examination" principle (the inability of
the enemies of Christianity to disprove its central claim
that Christ resurrected bodily from the dead in spite of
the motive and opportunity to do so)—all coalesce
directly or indirectly to support the preponderance of evidence for Christianity while the burden of proof proper
(the legal burden) for disproving it rests with the critic,
who, in 2000 years, has yet to make a case.[30]

The above seven facts—textual accuracy; archaeological confirmation; accurate reporting and conviction of
truth, especially that of Jesus Christ; extra-biblical cor-
roboration; numerous eyewitness accounts to the events;
critics' and skeptics' contributions; and additional log-
ical/legal considerations—*demonstrate* the reliability of
the Bible.

What this means is that we can trust what the biblical
authors say as being true.

7

Does biblical archaeology confirm
the reliability of the Bible?

Biblical archaeology does confirm the biblical record's
trustworthiness—greatly—primarily by demonstrating
that it is dependable whenever archaeological discoveries
come to bear on the biblical text. Obviously, archaeology
cannot be expected to confirm every statement of biblical
history, geography, culture, and so on because the amount
of information archaeology has uncovered is still relatively small. In addition, there are sometimes problems
with interpretation of the data.

The significant point is that when sufficient factual information becomes known, and is properly interpreted, it confirms the biblical record. In cases where a discovery initially seems not to confirm the Bible, sufficient factual data is never encountered in order to disprove a biblical statement. Given the thousands of minute details in the Bible that archaeology has the opportunity to disprove, this confirmation of the biblical record is striking. For example, by 1958 "over 25,000 sites from the biblical world have been confirmed by some archaeological discoveries to date."[31] Also, the 17-volume *Archaeology, the Bible and Christ* by Dr. Clifford Wilson, former Director of the Australian Institute of Archaeology in Melbourne, brings together more than 5000 facts relating archaeology to the Bible. He closes volume 17 by pointing out that "the Bible stands investigation in ways that are unique in all literature. Its superiority to attack, its capacity to withstand criticism, its amazing facility to be proved right after all are all staggering by any standards of scholarship. Seemingly assured results 'disproving' the Bible have a habit of backfiring. Over and over again the Bible has been vindicated. That is true from Genesis to Revelation, as we have seen in this book."[32]

The importance of archaeological data in confirmation of the biblical record is evident when we understand that material confirmation leads one to have confidence in the Bible's spiritual teachings. In other words, those who believe that the Bible is unreliable in historical matters can hardly be expected to accept its teachings in spiritual matters. To illustrate in a more mundane subject, a famous authors' cookbook may promise heavenly culinary delights, but if the recipe ingredients are wrong, it won't matter.

Concerning the Bible's spiritual teachings, when we add the words of the Gospel of Luke and the book of Acts, we discover that the physician Luke wrote fully one-fourth of the entire New Testament, and we earlier mentioned that his detailed accuracy was confirmed by modern archaeology. Significantly, it is this very same careful historian who reports that Jesus Christ was physically resurrected from the dead by "many convincing proofs" (Acts 1:3)—and that he had carefully investigated the evidence for this from the beginning (Luke 1:1-4). If Luke was so painstakingly accurate in his historical reporting, on what basis may we logically assume he was credulous or inaccurate in his reporting of matters that were far more important, not only to him but to everyone else as well? Luke's meticulous accuracy in historical, geographical, political, and cultural matters lends weight to his claims concerning the resurrection of Christ as well, even though he is dealing with an unparalleled miraculous event. Habitually vigilant and careful people such as responsible physicians do not go out on such a limb unless they are certain it will bear the weight demanded.

Considering the Old Testament, archaeology has vindicated the biblical record time and again. *The New International Dictionary of Biblical Archaeology*, written by a score of experts in various fields, repeatedly shows that biblical history is vindicated. To illustrate, the editor's preface remarks, "Near Eastern archaeology has demonstrated the historical and geographical reliability of the Bible in many important areas.... It is now known, for instance, that, along with the Hittites, Hebrew scribes were the *best historians in the entire ancient Near East*, despite contrary propaganda that emerged from Assyria, Egypt, and elsewhere."[33]

John Arthur Thompson was also director of the Australian Institute of Archaeology in Melbourne and has done archaeological fieldwork with the American Schools of Oriental Research. In *The Bible and Archaeology* he writes, "If one impression stands out more clearly than any other today, it is that on all hands the overall historicity of the Old Testament tradition is admitted."[34] Geisler and Brooks point out, "In every period of Old Testament history, we find that there is good evidence from archaeology that the scriptures are accurate.... While many have doubted the accuracy of the Bible, time and continued research have consistently demonstrated that the Word of God is better informed than its critics."[35]

The reliability of the New Testament is also confirmed by archaeological data: "The evidence for its historical reliability [is] overwhelming."[36] Historian and apologist Dr. John Warwick Montgomery summarizes the evidence when he writes, "Modern archaeological research has confirmed again and again the reliability of New Testament geography, chronology, and general history."[37]

There are, again, literally thousands of opportunities for archaeological research to indisputably prove the Bible false—and yet it has never done so! In a book (endorsed, incidentally, by an editorial board comprising American liberal clergymen), we read: "Nowhere has archaeological discovery refuted the Bible as history."[38] Probably the three greatest American archaeologists of the twentieth century (W.F. Albright, Nelson Glueck, and George Ernest Wright) each had their skeptical liberal training altered by their archaeological work, bolstering their confidence in the biblical text. Albright said of the Bible that "discovery after discovery has established the accuracy of innumerable details."[39] Glueck came to trust what he termed "the remarkable phenomenon of historical memory in the Bible" and forthrightly declared, "It may be clearly stated categorically that no archaeological discovery has ever controverted a single biblical reference."[40] How can we account for such a fact apart from divine inspiration?

Indeed, biblical archaeology continues to offer migraines to Bible critics. This statement by Assyriologist A.H. Sayce made in the early part of the last century continues to hold true today: "Time after time the most positive assertions of a skeptical criticism have been disproved by archaeological discovery, events and personages that were confidently pronounced to be mythical have been shown to be historical, and the older [i.e., biblical] writers have turned out to have been better acquainted with what they were describing than the modern critic who has flouted them."[41] Millar Burrows of Yale points out that "archaeology has in many cases refuted the views of modern critics. It has been shown in a number of instances that these views rest on false assumptions and unreal, artificial schemes of historical development," and "the excessive skepticism of many liberal theologians stems not from a careful evaluation of the available data, but from an enormous predisposition against the supernatural."[42] Finally, the noted classical scholar Professor E.M. Blaiklock once wrote, quite correctly, "Recent archaeology has destroyed much nonsense and will destroy more. And I use the word nonsense deliberately, for theories and speculations find currency in biblical scholarship that would not be tolerated for a moment in any other branch of literary or historical criticism."[43]

The double standard of skeptical critical scholarship at this point is illustrated in its double-minded approach. On the one hand, anytime archaeology does not directly confirm something the Bible teaches, the tendency is to allege an error. On the other hand, critics frequently tend to avoid using archaeology whenever it confirms the Bible.[44] Indeed, when one looks at the archaeological negation of the dominant liberal theories and methods in biblical studies, such as the documentary hypothesis of the Pentateuch, the alleged "Q" source for the New Testament, and form criticism,[45] it may surprise no one that critics have ignored archaeology when it discredits theories that they have held to for personal rather than valid reasons.

8

What about alleged Bible errors and contradictions?

Far too many people have uncritically accepted the claims of skeptics that the biblical accounts have errors or conflict, are thus unreliable, and that therefore the Bible itself should not be trusted. The vast majority of alleged contradictions result from three factors: 1) hasty or casual examination of the text; 2) the faulty assumptions and methods of the critics; and 3) the authors' selective use of data. Careful analysis invariably reveals an error or contradiction does not exist. Thus, when basic principles for dealing with alleged errors or discrepancies are followed, the great majority of claimed problems are resolved merely by a judicious evaluation of the biblical text itself.[46]

First, the proper definitions of "contradiction" and "error" must be observed. Many who write on these subjects carve errors themselves because they do not understand or follow the dictionary meaning of these terms.

Second, rather than presuppose error, or worse, fraud, impartial critical scholarship would assume the writer is being honest *until* proven otherwise, even when one does not like his conclusions. Thus, the limitations on human knowledge should be granted; no critic is omniscient, and none have perfect knowledge. But in a book the age and size of the Bible, repeated confirmation of the text would hopefully tell one something. In other words, every alleged error or contradiction in Scripture has been proven a truthful statement once sufficient archaeological or other information has been discovered. This gives one full confidence that problems currently unresolvable for lack of data will eventually have a similar outcome. Too often, however, critics don't get the message.

Third, first impressions can be deceptive. Unless one understands what an author has actually said, one will be incapable of interpreting him properly. Serious study must be given to all relevant areas: original languages, history, literary form, immediate and larger contexts, geography, culture, sound principles of literary interpretation, archaeological data, specialized use of terms, and so on (e.g., principles of interpretation that apply to one literary form do not always apply to another). In fact, the large majority of apparent errors and contradictions result precisely from omitting this principle. For example, the works of Drs. John W. Haley, William Arndt, and Gleason Archer collectively examine over a thousand alleged Bible errors and contradictions, almost all of which are adequately resolved by careful attention to relevant detail.[47]

Fourth, mere differences do not constitute contradictions. Writers have the right to select those facts that fit their purposes and to disregard others. Critics who will not accept this principle are applying a standard to the biblical writers that they would apply to no one else, themselves included.

Fifth, critics need to reexamine their own biases and the validity of their critical theories and methods, whether the documentary hypothesis of Moses' writings, the late date (165 B.C.) for Daniel, multiple authors for Isaiah, the assumption of proven contradictions in the differing resurrection accounts, form and redaction criticism, and on and on. Put simply, critics don't seem to like most biblical books because they claim to be revelations from God and contain amazing predictions of the future, something critics rule out as impossible to begin with. Rather than accept even the possibility of divine revelation, it seems skeptics would prefer to spend vast amounts of time defending artificial speculations and imaginings.

Indeed, for ages critics have proposed their theories—and yet such theories have never marshaled legitimate evidence in their support. They are speculations plucked out of the air for personal and philosophical reasons, not because textual, historical, archaeological, or other data suggest they are true—to the contrary. The actual data are solidly on the side of the Bible, not the critics, as numerous scholarly and popular texts have demonstrated.[48] Indeed, what K.A. Kitchen declares of the dominant critical theory on the books of Moses, termed the documentary hypothesis, is true for critical theories generally—despite their widespread acceptance in intellectual circles: "Even the most ardent advocate of the documentary theory must admit that we have as yet *no single scrap* of external, objective *material* [i.e., tangible] evidence for either the existence or the history of 'J,' 'E', or any other alleged source-document."[49]

In sum, the fair use of critical scholarship will support the trustworthiness of the Bible—it's just a shame that it is so infrequently employed.

The information discussed to date should help us to take more seriously the Bible's claim to inerrancy, or being without error, which is something unique among all the ancient books of the world and a fact that can only be explained through divine revelation. In effect, God wrote the Bible. That's why we should carefully listen to it.

9

Does biblical data per se prove the Bible is without error?

Modern scientific rationalism has explained very little of the heights and depths of the universe. To declare absolutely that inerrant inspiration is impossible is itself impossible unless one is God and has the omniscience to be absolutely certain of the impossibility. It is mere speculation to assume that an infinite personal God could never communicate His revelation truthfully. In fact, in light of the biblical data and 2000 years of critical biblical research, it becomes simple arrogance to make such a declaration.

Inerrancy cannot be 100 percent factually proven only because our knowledge and interpretation are not 100 percent perfect. If they were, based on all the evidence to date, there is every reason to believe inerrancy would be demonstrated. This is why many leading scholars concur that the alleged problems critics say confront inerrancy aren't problems at all. Dr. John Warwick Montgomery: "I myself have never encountered an alleged contradiction in the Bible which could not be cleared up by the use of the original languages of the Scriptures and/or by the use of accepted principles of literary and historical interpretation."[50] Dr. Gleason L. Archer: "As I have dealt with one apparent discrepancy after another and have studied the alleged contradictions between the biblical record and the evidence of linguistics, archaeology, or science, my confidence in the trustworthiness of Scripture has been repeatedly verified and strengthened by the discovery that almost every problem in Scripture that has ever been discovered by man, from ancient times until now, has been dealt with in a completely satisfactory manner by the biblical text itself—or else by objective archaeological information."[51] Dr. Robert Dick Wilson: "I have made it an invariable habit never to accept an objection to a statement of the Old Testament without subjecting it to a most thorough investigation, linguistically and factually," and "I defy any man to make an attack upon the Old Testament on the grounds of evidence that I cannot investigate." His conclusion was that no critic has succeeded in proving an error in the Old Testament.[52] Dr. William Arndt concluded in his own study of alleged contradictions and errors in the Bible with: "[W]e may say with full conviction that no instances of this sort occur anywhere in the Scriptures."[53]

The burden of proof always rests with the one who alleges error. What critics have never successfully dealt with is the fact that in 3000 years an error has never been proven in the Bible—just one more miracle of the Bible critics are unwilling to concede. Errors are assumed merely because it is convenient to assume them.

We stress again, given the phenomena of Scripture in general, that the biblical text should at least be considered innocent until proven guilty. If men are presumed innocent until proven guilty, how is it we presume God—after He supplies sufficient evidence for belief—is still pronounced guilty?

The conclusion is that someone must be the judge of Scripture. Either it must be God, who has already borne witness to its authority and inerrancy (Isaiah 40:8; John 5:46-47;10:35) or it must be critics who judge God to be in error. Skeptics somehow assume error where Jesus declares truth; somehow assert the superiority of finite and fallible human reason above divine revelation, somehow assume the legitimacy of theory and myth over fact. Regrettably, in that they establish an authoritative criterion above that of God Himself, they commit a form of idolatry. In essence, they carve an idol from their own minds and worship it devotedly.

10

Does prophecy prove the Bible is God's only revelation to man?

If only one religious scripture on earth has specific predictions of the future, then it would seem that such scripture alone comprises a divine revelation. Indeed, a central purpose of biblical prophecy is just this—to reveal the one true God "so that all the peoples of the earth may know that the LORD is God and that there is no other" (1 Kings 8:60; cf. verses 1-59). God teaches that His knowledge of the future is proof that He alone is the Lord. No one else has consistently told of things to come and also had them come true exactly as forecast (see Isaiah 41:20-29). God did this "so that people may see and know, may consider and understand, that the hand of the LORD has done this" (Isaiah 41:20). God challenges men to put Him to the test so that even the skeptics and stubborn-hearted will have no excuse for rejecting Him (Isaiah 48:3-7).

The reason we know that biblical prophecies are genuine is because they are given by God Himself. "All Scripture is inspired by God" (2 Timothy 3:16 NASB); "Prophecy never had its origin in the will of man, but men spoke from God as they were carried along by the Holy Spirit" (2 Peter 1:21). In fact, God promises 100 percent reliability in His predictions of the future, and He has done so in order that people may know that He alone is the one true God: "Whatever I say will be fulfilled, declares the Sovereign LORD" (Ezekiel 12:28). His prophets are "recognized as one truly sent by the LORD only if [their] prediction comes true" (Jeremiah 28:9; cf. Deuteronomy 18:21-22).

Again, totally accurate prediction of the future is the domain of the Bible exclusively—and one of the great proofs of its exclusive divine origin. Approximately 27 percent of the entire Bible contains prophetic material—an astonishing figure for so large a book. Prophecies are found in 62 of the 66 books of the Bible. According to a standard encyclopedia on the subject: "[O]f the OT's 23,210 verses, 6,641 contain predictive material, or 28½ percent. Out of the NT's 7,914 verses, 1,711 contain predictive material, or 21½ percent. So for the entire Bible's 31,124 verses, 8,352 contain predictive material, or 27 percent of the whole."[54] Of these, about 22 percent, more than 1800 verses (including 318 in the New Testament) deal with the *Second* Coming of Christ.[55] If this means anything, it means that the physical return of Jesus Christ to the earth has the same chance of being fulfilled as all of the other prophecies—100 percent.[56]

Consider these examples of fulfilled prophecy:

King Josiah—In a prophecy to King Jeroboam (930–909 B.C.), 1 Kings 13:2 predicted King Josiah by name and lineage 300 *years* before he was ever born: "This is what the LORD says: 'A son named Josiah will be born to the house of David…'" Josiah was a contemporary of Pharoah Neco, King of Egypt (610–595 B.C.; 2 Kings 23:29). God also predicted that this king would destroy the altar at Bethel after sacrificing the evil prophets and burning their bones upon it. All this happened exactly as was prophesied—300 years later (see 2 Kings 23:14-19).

Bethlehem—The prophet Micah predicted by name the very town and region of the birthplace of the Messiah, Jesus, 700 years in advance, also predicted to be eternal and the ruler of Israel. "But as for you, Bethlehem Ephrathah [Ephrathah is the region in which Bethlehem was located]...from you One will go forth for Me to be ruler in Israel. His goings forth are from long ago, from the days of eternity" (Micah 5:2 NASB).

The Babylonian Captivity—No one can reasonably deny that the internal and external evidence in the book of Isaiah proves Isaiah was written approximately 700–680 B.C.[57] The book of Isaiah was definitely in existence 100 years before the Babylonian captivity of the Jews, which began in 605 B.C. Yet in Isaiah 39:5-7, we find the Babylonian captivity itself predicted: "Then Isaiah said to Hezekiah, 'Hear the word of the LORD Almighty: The time will surely come when everything in your palace, and all that your fathers have stored up until this day, will be carried off to Babylon. Nothing will be left, says the LORD. And some of your descendants, your own flesh and blood who will be born to you, will be taken away, and they will become eunuchs in the palace of the King of Babylon' " (see Daniel 1:1-3).

Future Kingdoms—The internal and external evidence demand a sixth century (530) B.C. composition for the book of Daniel. Yet the prophet Daniel (Matthew 24:15) predicts the Medo-Persian, Greek, and Roman Empires (chapters 2, 7, 8) in such detail that anti-supernaturalists are forced, against all the evidence, to date the book at 165 B.C., implying it is essentially a forgery.[58]

King Cyrus—Isaiah predicted a very important Persian king by name 120 years before he was born. The prophet predicted King Cyrus as the one who would permit the Jews to return to their land after the Babylonian captivity (Isaiah 44:24–45:6). Once again, the reason God does this is so man will understand and know that He alone is the one true God: "This is what the LORD says to his anointed, to Cyrus, whose right hand I take hold of to subdue nations before him...so that you may know that I am the LORD, the God of Israel, who summons you by name...I am the LORD, and there is no other; apart from me there is no God" (Isaiah 45:1,3,5). Ezra records the fulfillment of this prophecy in chapter 1 of his book, referring to related prophecies in Jeremiah (Ezra 1:1-11; cf. Jeremiah 25:11-12; 29:10-14).

Messianic Prophecy—Finally, consider a small sampling of Jesus' fulfillment of exact Old Testament Messianic prophecies—how can these possibly be accounted for apart from divine foreknowledge?

1. He would be born of a virgin (Isaiah 7:14; Matthew 1:23).

2. He would live in Nazareth of Galilee (Isaiah 9:1-2; Matthew 2:22-23; 4:15).

3. He would occasion the massacre of Bethlehem's children (Jeremiah 31:15; Matthew 2:16-18).

4. His mission would unexpectedly include the Gentiles (Isaiah 42:1-3,6; Matthew 12:18-21), and He would unexpectedly be rejected by the Jews, His own people (Psalm 118:22; 1 Peter 2:7).

5. His ministry would include miracles (Isaiah 35:1-6; 61:1-2; Matthew 9:35; Luke 4:16-21), and He would be the Shepherd struck with the sword, resulting in the sheep being scattered (Zechariah 13:7; Matthew 26:31,56; Mark 14:27,49-50).

6. He would be betrayed by a friend for 30 pieces of silver (Zechariah 11:12-13; Matthew 27:7-10).

7. He would die a humiliating death (Psalm 22; Isaiah 53), including rejection (Isaiah 53:3; John 1:10-11; 7:5,48); silence before His accusers (Isaiah 53:7; Matthew 27:12-14); being mocked (Psalm 22:7; Matthew 27:31); the piercing of His hands and feet (Psalm 22:16; Luke 23:33); being crucified with thieves (Isaiah 53:12; Matthew 27:38) yet praying for His persecutors (Isaiah 53:12; Luke 23:43); having lots cast for His garments (Psalm 22:18; John 19:23-24); the piercing of His side (Zechariah 12:10; John 19:34); being given vinegar and gall to drink (Psalm 69:21; Matthew 27:34); and being buried in a rich man's tomb (Isaiah 53:9; Matthew 27:57-60). He would also rise from the dead (Psalm 16:10; Mark 16:6; Acts 2:31); ascend into heaven (Psalm 68:18; Acts 1:9), and sit down at God's right hand (Psalm 110:1; Hebrews 1:3).[59]

Some 1800 prophecies in the Bible are logically best explained by divine foreknowledge and no other reason. Even skeptics will admit that specific predicting of the future is a miracle, so perhaps skeptics should reconsider their premises.[60]

11

What can skeptics learn from science and mathematics about the Bible?

Over the years we have had various skeptics and critics of the Bible on *The John Ankerberg Show*. Neither from the guests on our TV show or our reading of the skeptical literature have we ever found a legitimate argument against the Bible that would stand the weight of scrutiny. Skeptics generally don't believe the Bible simply because they don't want to believe it. How do we know this? Because historically thousands of former skeptics have become Christians on the *basis* of the evidence. If that evidence didn't exist or weren't persuasive, these former skeptics would never have become Christians. While no amount of evidence will convince someone against his will, for the open-minded the evidence is more than sufficient to establish belief.

Two areas in particular that may interest open-minded skeptics are the scientific prevision found in the Bible and the mathematical factors in favor of its divine inspiration as seen through prophecy. Concerning the scientific prevision of the Bible, this is once again something unique in the history of religious literature. In *The Creator Beyond Time and Space*, Mark Eastman, M.D., and Chuck Missler, a computer specialist, provide many examples showing how the Bible, scientifically speaking, was thousands of years ahead of its time. They point out that "there are dozens of passages in the Bible which demonstrate tremendous scientific foreknowledge."[61] And, "when the biblical text is carefully examined the reader will quickly discover an uncanny scientific accuracy unparalled by any document of antiquity.... In virtually all ancient religious documents it is common to find scientifically inaccurate myths about the nature of the universe and the life forms on planet earth.... However...throughout the Bible we find scientifically accurate concepts about the physical universe that were not 'discovered' by modern scientists until very recent times."[62]

For skeptics to successfully maintain that the Bible is not the inspired Word of God, they must explain how the

Bible contains accurate scientific information that was often disharmonious with the accepted knowledge of the time. "To argue that the evidence for biblical inspiration is the result of a myriad of lucky guesses requires an enormous measure of faith"[63] because we know that it is impossible for people to write science and history in advance apart from divine inspiration.

Another primary example is *The Biblical Basis for Modern Science*, in which scientist Dr. Henry Morris, author of dozens of books on the Bible and science, offers a 500-page text supplying a large number of additional examples of scientific foreknowledge or allusions in the Bible. In the above two books, examples are provided from physics, astronomy, oceanography, the earth's hydrologic cycle, meteorology, medicine, geology, and biology.

In sum, many leading scientists have been very impressed by the scientific accuracy of the Bible. One of them was the late A.E. Wilder-Smith, who held three earned doctorates in science and was the author of numerous popular and technical books and scientific papers, including *The Natural Sciences Know Nothing of Evolution*, *He Who Thinks Has to Believe*, and *The Creation of Life*. In *The Reliability of the Bible*, Dr. Wilder-Smith discussed the historic and prophetic accuracy of Scripture and wrote, commenting upon those with initial doubts about the scientific accuracy of the Bible, "Many leading scientists and philosophers, past and present, accepted the entire Bible because they actually researched these matters."[64] The presence of error in ancient books can be expected; the false assumption was that the Bible is like any other book. In other words, once these men really examined what the Bible had to say, they found their doubts faded and they became convinced of the historic, prophetic, and scientific accuracy of the Bible. As Eastman and Missler conclude, "In the twentieth century, more than any time in history, it can be demonstrated that the Bible is a skillfully designed, integrated message system that evidences supernatural engineering in every detail."[65]

When we examine biblical prophecy and mathematical probabilities, we find even more powerful evidence that the Bible must be considered the Word of God. For God to have promised His predictions were 100 percent accurate and then offered 8352 predictive verses in the Bible, including 1817 total predictions with 737 separate matters forecast, consider how unbelievably easy it would be to prove the Bible were not the Word of God just by finding a single false prediction. But no false prediction has ever been proven.

When we consider messianic prophecy alone, we see that the odds against natural fulfillment are astronomical—literally impossible—and yet messianic prophecy is only a small part of the overall prophetic record in the Bible. The number of messianic predictions from which to choose is large: Smith discusses 73, Payne more than 125, and Edersheim more than 400.[66] That neither Jesus nor anyone else could have arranged to fulfill these prophecies is obvious because it is impossible for people to arrange such things as being born in a specific family; having one's parents give birth to oneself in a specific town that is not their own city; to arrange one's own death with specific details that are beyond one's ability to orchestrate, such as arranging one's betrayal for a specific amount of money (30 pieces of silver); and having one's executioners gamble for one's clothes during execution by crucifixion.

Former Professor Emeritus of Science at Westmont College, Peter Stoner, calculated the probability of one man fulfilling just eight major prophecies made concerning the Messiah. The estimates were worked out by 12 different classes of 600 college students. Stoner took their estimates and made them considerably more conservative. He encouraged skeptics or other scientists to make their own estimates to see if his conclusions were fair. Then he submitted his figures for review to a committee of the American Scientific Affiliation, which verified his calculations "were accurate in regard to the scientific material presented."[67]

The very conservative chance of one man fulfilling all eight prophecies was 1 in 10^{17}, or 1 chance in 100,000 trillion (100,000,000,000,000,000.) In another calculation, Professor Stoner used 48 prophecies and arrived at the extremely conservative estimate that the probability of 48 prophecies being fulfilled in one person is 10^{157},[68] for all practical purposes an infinitely larger figure than one chance in 10^{17}.

Here's a brief illustration of the immensity of the number 10^{157} and why the science of probability powerfully proves we can only be dealing with the miraculous. Imagine an ant. This ant has such severe arthritis it takes him 15 billion years just to travel *one inch*. His job is to carry a single atom on his back trillions and trillions of miles into space, and then return for one more atom. If he could carry only one atom at a time, how long would it take him to carry *all* the atoms in our universe trillions of miles into space? Our little pain-ridden ant, even at his depressingly slow speed, could actually move *all* the atoms in our universe in 10^{157} years. Incidentally, just the atoms in the letters of this sentence are trillions and trillions, so you can image how long it would take him to carry just one letter trillions of miles, let alone an entire universe. But he could carry not just the atoms in *our* universe, but in 600,000 trillion, trillion, trillion, trillion universes like ours. And he could actually carry them a distance of 30 billion light years, i.e., endless trillions of miles into outer space, even to the known end of the universe and far, far beyond—*one atom at a time*—in 10^{157} years! That gives one a small idea of the immensity of the number 10^{157}.[69] In addition, as shown technically by Emile Borel (*Probabilities and Life*) and William Dembsky (*The Design Inference*), one "chance" in 10^{157} is actually no chance at all, ever. The "probability" is absolute zero.[70] This illustrates that it is virtually impossible for these 48 prophecies to be fulfilled by chance alone. If no one in the world would bet their life savings on a horse race with odds of one chance in a million, how is it that so many bet their convictions about reality, with far more sober consequence if wrong, on odds infinitely worse?

Then again, what of the 1800 prophecies in the Bible, not just 48? All this is proof that there must be a God who supernaturally gave this information, and that He alone is the true God.

What can skeptics learn from prophecy, science, and mathematics about the Bible? Perhaps the most truthful and stimulating statement of all: There is a God who can be known.

SECTION III

The Responsibility of Historical Research

12

What is rationalistic biblical criticism, and how do we distinguish it from valid historical research?

Legitimate historical research attempts to be objective and reasonable, to be fair and to keep unwarranted speculation to a minimum, and to disallow unjustified presuppositions to color one's conclusions. Rationalistic biblical criticism on the other hand, also known as "higher" biblical criticism, such as form and redaction approaches, involves a particular attitude to the biblical text where unfounded assumptions and biases prevent a researcher from dealing fairly with biblical material. Presuppositions, of course, are not proven facts, and the philosophical, historical, or scientific assumptions underlying higher criticism are far from sound.[71] (E.g., scientific naturalism, rationalism, and evolutionism.)

Perhaps the most flawed basic assumption is that miracles are impossible, so they never happen. If that is true, then the Bible cannot be divinely inspired, for this would be a miracle. In addition, all the supernatural miracles recorded in the Bible, from Moses through the prophets to Jesus and the apostles, are obviously fraudulent since miracles never occur. And, of course, Jesus never rose from the dead, so Christianity itself is based upon a powerful deception, however well intended it might otherwise be.

While there is clearly value to objective critical research, especially textual criticism, which has vindicated the biblical text, inherently biased critical methods are of almost no historical value. While some critical methods are neutral, many are not.

To illustrate, an article at www.infidels.org claimed to present a more balanced middle-of-the-road approach to biblical criticism and to avoid the frequent biases one encounters. Yet in "Critique of New Testament Reliability and 'Bias' in NT Development," we find incredible statements. These illustrate the author is as biased as anyone, allowing his premises to form his conclusions without looking reasonably at all the biblical, historical,

44

and textual data. Without a shred of evidence he assumes there was a "Q" source (see below), that the Gospels could *not* be fully reliable historically, that the early church invented Jesus as a divine savior, and so on: "...early Christians pictured Jesus as a magician..." "...the NT texts...changed so much over the centuries..." "the gospels...are not first-hand accounts of his [Jesus'] deeds and activities..." "All four of the gospels are pseudepigraphical works and today we use the names 'Matthew' or 'John' merely as convenient labels for the work..." "...the post-Easter Christ which is taught today is far different from the real wandering rabbi and Jewish peasant of first-century Palestine..." "...the Q material is present in nearly 200 verses in both Matthew and Luke."[72]

Based on the facts we have, such conclusions are not only historically irresponsible, they are nonsense. And this is the problem of so much biblical "scholarship" today—it can be likened to a thirsty man finding a well of poisoned water in the desert—useless, disappointing, and dangerous all at once.

The above author is simply employing *radical form* criticism, beginning with the baseless premise that the biblical books constitute a later and adulterated written form of oral teachings that had earlier been circulated. By the time this oral tradition was written down, a great deal of deceptive alteration had occurred. Most of this deviation resulted from the inventive *imagination* of early Christians. In the end, form criticism concludes that most of what we find in the Bible is largely myth rather than history. *Redaction* criticism builds directly upon radical form criticism. It is almost entirely a biased and subversive methodology. It assumes without any evidence that the findings of radical form criticism are legitimate and then extends the assumptions of Christian invention and myth even further. Redaction critics also attempt to uncover the theological *motivation* of an author, which leads to all sorts of irrelevant speculation.[73]

The biased or radical forms of literary, historical, and form criticism, plus redaction criticism, are often utilized together. The end result permits the critic or skeptic to sit in judgment on Scripture and, by fanciful whim alone, determine what he will or will not accept—so guesswork and individual bias dominate any investigation. The conclusion of these critical methodologies, pure and simple, is that Christianity is a fraud. If so, we can make Jesus anyone we want Him to be.

We suggested earlier that rationalistic critics and theologians generally, despite their claims, were not
searchers after the truth. If they were, Jesus Himself tells
us they would *listen* to His words rather than discredit
them. "In fact, for this reason I was born, and for this I
came into the world, to testify to *the truth*. Everyone on
the side of truth *listens to me*" (John 18:37, emphasis
added). Jesus said, "I *am*...the truth" (John 14:6,
emphasis added) and "Thy *word* is truth" (John 17:17
KJV, emphasis added).

In the name of discovering truth, what we discover is
that the real myth makers are the critics of the Bible. We
can know this because the conclusions drawn by higher
criticism are *demonstrably false* and yet broadcast far and
wide and defended regardless. For example, it is logically
impossible to believe the basic assumption of any criticism which, in effect, attributes to a first-century, scattered Christian community the kind of creative power to
fabricate the Jesus Christ of the New Testament. This is
either unbelievable, absurd, or both:

> ...with regard to the discourses attributed to Jesus, it
> should at once be realized that a community cannot
> create such sayings. We know from experience that a
> saying must come originally from an individual. A com-
> munity can only adopt, transmit, and preserve a saying,
> but the saying itself must first exist. Now the sayings
> attributed to Jesus in the gospels are by common con-
> sent of a singular nobility, loftiness, and power; elevated
> in character and style. If it be held that in some way
> the Christian community originated these discourses
> and statements, then it must follow, as scholar Burton
> Scott Easton argues, that the Palestinian church either
> had in its midst a single, brilliant thinker "from whom
> the sayings all proceeded, but whose name and very exis-
> tence has disappeared from history—something well-
> nigh unthinkable—or else there were a number of gifted
> individuals all fired with the same superlative genius
> and all endowed with the same exquisite style—an even
> more difficult conception."

> The simple fact is that there is not the slightest indi-
> cation in New Testament or secular history of the exis-
> tence of such an anonymous, dynamic, prophetic leader,
> who would surely be greater and wiser even than ancient
> Solomon; or of a group of such leaders, gifted with the
> capacity of creating original discourses such as are found
> in the gospels. The only plausible explanation for these

sayings is that they originated, as the evangelists declare, with Jesus; the life situation from which they stem is assuredly to be found in Jesus Himself.[74]

Indeed, the more we carefully examine negative criticism generally, the more difficult it is to accept its conclusions. It reminds us of the situation with the naturalistic explanations for the origin of life or the physical resurrection of Christ—*all* are much harder to believe than the miracle of creation or the resurrection itself. In similar fashion, critical approaches and their logical conclusions are far more difficult to believe than what the New Testament plainly teaches. If what the critics say were true, there never would have been a religion of Christianity to begin with, as we demonstrated elsewhere.[75] Given the Jewish origin of Christianity, only Christ's resurrection could have provided the stimulus for Christian beginnings, because Jesus' teachings would have been proven fraudulent unless He rose physically from the dead, and His followers would have continued their abandonment of Him. The first 25,000 or so Christians were all Jews who, based exclusively on Christ's resurrection, radically revised sacred and inviolate Jewish institutions—e.g., discarding animal sacrifice, eliminating legalistic keeping of the Sabbath, which actually changed to Sunday, rejecting the Mosaic Law as a means of salvation, a theology of Unitarian monotheism altered to trinitarianism, and so on. Such powerful and immutable institutions could never have been revised *by Jews* apart from the resurrection of Christ. In essence, the mere fact that Christianity exists is disproof of the critics' theories. In the end, our only options are to believe in the folly of a critical methodology and its myths or in the soundness of what the Bible teaches. Proof of this is further illustrated in the next question.

13

Are rationalistic critical approaches such as the Jesus Seminar and "Q" studies just nonsense?

As we have seen, the difficulty is not with what the Bible teaches, but with the critical theories themselves, which encompass numerous historic errors, internal contradictions, reversals of position, blatant ignoring of contrary data, special pleading, and so on. When, upon the flimsiest of grounds, critics reject the Bible that Jesus authenticated on unassailable grounds, they only reveal their own ignorance, somehow assuming they are wiser than Jesus. For hundreds of years in biblical studies, scholars have had little problem finding what they wrongly assume, somehow never questioning the frailty of their own assumptions.

The Jesus Seminar and the reliance upon the alleged "Q" source aptly illustrate the unfortunate methods of liberal critical biblical scholarship generally. In 1993, the conclusions of the Jesus Seminar were published in a large, detailed text titled *The Five Gospels: The Search for the Authentic Words of Jesus.* It reduces Jesus' fully authentic words in the Gospels to less than six percent of what is recorded! In other words, 94 percent of what we read Jesus saying in the Gospels has some degree of doubt or is just plain wrong. "Eight-two percent of the words ascribed to Jesus in the gospels were not actually spoken by him."[76] The Gospel of Mark, for example, had only *one* single verse of over 280 verses definitely spoken by Jesus—Mark 12:17. This means that Mark (or, supposedly, Christian tradition) misquoted or invented the words of Jesus some 300 times for every time he quoted Jesus correctly. And worse (if that were possible), virtually *everything* in the Gospel of John was voted unreliable! This is scholarly prejudice driven to the point of absurdity.

Three of the many key errors made by the Jesus Seminar are:

1. The false claim that its conclusions represent a consensus of modern scholarship—e.g., the views of 70 terribly biased rationalistic critics can hardly be considered representative of the 7000 members of the Society of Biblical Literature (SBL) or thousands of others.

2. Its deliberate skepticism and prejudice, which are entirely without justification—e.g., its premeditated agenda to discredit people's trust in the Gospels *despite* their being established as historically reliable. One reads with astonishment, "The evidence provided by the written gospels is hearsay evidence. Hearsay evidence is secondhand evidence…none of them [the Gospel authors] was an ear or eyewitness of the words and events he records."[77] Of course, if one arbitrarily discards the great majority of the Gospels as unreliable, one is unlikely to trust claims to being

an eyewitness, such as that of the apostle John in his Gospel (21:24) and Epistle: "That which was from the beginning, which we have heard, which we have seen with our eyes, which we have looked at and our hands have touched—this we proclaim.... We proclaim to you what we have seen and heard" (1 John 1:1,3). Indeed in the Gospel of John, the noun "witness" or "testimony" and the verb "testify" are used almost 50 times—no wonder the Jesus Seminar so thoroughly discarded it (cf., Luke 1:2; 24:48; Hebrews 2:3; 1 Peter 5:1; John 3:11; 5:36; 19:35; 21:24; Acts 2:32; 3:15; 5:32; 10:39; 26:26; 1 John 4:14; 5:9-10).

3. Serious and/or fatal methodological flaws that tear down their own premises and conclusions—such as their naturalistic bias and hostility toward biblical faith. For example, the Jesus Seminar's claims to impartiality and using legal standards of evidence are highly misleading. The truth is that their so-called "rules" of investigation are frequently irrelevant and/or incorporate their own biases against the text so that *applying* the rules only proves the critical conclusions already held. Thus, their context rule *assumes* without justification that the Gospel writers "*invent[ed]* new narrative contexts" for the sayings of Jesus.[78] Or: "The Christ creed and dogma...can no longer command the assent of those who have seen the heavens through Galileo's telescope. The old deities and demons were swept from the skies.... [Science has] dismantled the mythological abodes of the gods and Satan, and bequeathed us secular heavens."[79] When the JS condescendingly disparages conservative Christians as "far right fundamentalists," "latter-day inquisitors," and "witch-hunters" and then claims "their reading of who Jesus was rests on the shifting sands of their own theological constructions," one can only stand in wonder at the hubris.[80] Unfortunately, the scholars of the Jesus Seminar care nothing for objective historical inquiry, let alone truth.

To illustrate more untamed speculation based on microscopic evidence, consider the collection of nonexistent Jesus sayings termed "Q" (supposedly used by Matthew, Mark, and Luke). Liberal scholars such as Burton Mack in *Who Wrote the New Testament?: The Making of the Christian Myth* (1995) are now speaking of Q1, Q2, Q3, and Q4 which, Johnson correctly points out, is preposterous and explains "why so much of contemporary New Testament scholarship is viewed with derision by mainstream historians. The entire edifice is 'a house of cards'.... Pull out one element and the whole construction crumbles."[81]

John Wenham has had a distinguished academic career as vice principal of Tyndale Hall, Bristol, lecturer in New Testament Greek at Bristol University, and warden of Latimer House, Oxford. He is the author of such important works as *Christ and the Bible* and *The Goodness of God*. In *Redating Matthew, Mark and Luke*, in which he dates the synoptics at 40, 45, and 54 respectively, he illustrates the quandary of biased critics. Wenham quotes M.D. Goulder, who writes, "Not tens but hundreds of thousands of pages have been wasted by authors on this Synoptic Problem [i.e., the likenesses and differences between the first three gospels] by not paying attention to errors of method." Wenham goes on to comment that "much of the argumentation is worth very little, because so many of the arguments are reversible: they can be argued either way with approximately equal cogency."[82] "Q" illustrates the quagmire scholars get themselves into when they are unwilling to take the text at face value even though there is every reason to do so. "Q" doesn't even *exist*, yet literally millions of man-hours have been consumed dissecting it! This is illustrated in the International "Q" Project's database research, which contains, for example, a 90-page single-spaced analysis of a *single* verse from Matthew—that was ultimately decided *not* to be "Q"![83]

As in the Jesus Seminar, the kind of scholarly speculation and/or nonsense represented by "Q" is irritating. Why emphasize the detailed study of something that doesn't exist, when what *does* exist is both authentic and accurate? Yet the "Q" project intends to publish more than 60 300-page volumes painstakingly evaluating its make-believe text! Each 300-page volume will deal with about 100 "words" from "Q"; per volume, that's three *pages* of scholarly analysis and discussion for every nonexistent *word* of "Q."[84] Somehow, critics demand we reject as myth the supposed "inventive imaginations" of the early Christians as to a reliable portrait of Jesus, but then they turn around and demand we accept their own conjured reconstructions as literal "gospel." No double standard here. Wenham says of "Q": "When we try to put the Q-theory to the test the matter is of course complicated by the fact that we have no text of Q to work with.... S.

Petrie in his *Novum Testamentum* 3 (1959) article, ' "Q" is Only What You Make It' has shown this in a colourful way. He speaks of the 'exasperating contradictoriness' of scholarly views as to its nature:

> 'Q' is a single document; it is a composite document, incorporating earlier sources; it is used in different redactions; it is more than one document. The original language of 'Q' is Greek; the original language is Aramaic; it is used in different translations. 'Q' is the Matthean Logia; it is not the Matthean Logia. 'Q' has a definite shape; it is no more than an amorphous collection of fragments. 'Q' is a gospel; it is not a gospel. "Q" includes the Crucifixion story; it does not include the Crucifixion story. 'Q' consists wholly of sayings and there is no narrative; it includes some narrative. All of 'Q' is preserved in Matt. and Luke; not all of it is preserved; it is better preserved in Luke. Matt.'s order is the correct order; Luke's is the correct order; neither order is correct. 'Q' is used by Mark; it is not used by Mark."[85]

It seems clear that critical scholars have used inventive theories like "Q" only to make Jesus into an image they are comfortable with—whether political revolutionary, mistaken Jewish sage, mystic, cynic, proto-feminist, and so on. Thus, Jesus' death and resurrection play no role in "Q's" understanding of salvation, which is clearly more gnostic than biblical. We also see "Q" appropriated by the Jesus Seminar "in their ongoing enterprise of 'dismantling the church's canon.' "[86] As Mack argues, "The remarkable thing about the people of Q is that they were not Christians. They did not think of Jesus as a Messiah. They did not regard his death as a...saving event...they did not imagine that he had been raised from the dead."[87]

It seems every other image of Jesus is currently acceptable to critics—except the one in the New Testament. Given the stated goal of discrediting orthodox Christianity, such a hopeless state of affairs is not surprising.

The reason for the critical conclusions should be obvious: If we accept the actual Jesus of history, the Jesus of the New Testament, then He is not only our Lord and Savior but our final Judge as well. He is not someone we may trifle with at our whim, but the One we must bow to as our Sovereign. We may sit in judgment upon Him now, but apart from repentance, it is He who will sit in judgment upon us later. Since the human heart, in its rebellion, prefers any thought but this, the almost desperate nature of the offensive "scholarship" to formulate a new Jesus is understandable. Once the biblical Jesus is adequately "disposed" of, we need not worry about the present or the future. It's kind of like taking your bank account to Vegas.

14

What are liberal theologians responsible for?

Lest we think this is all just academic debating, consider the tragic event relayed by William Lane Craig in *The Son Rises*, an excellent text on the historical evidence for Christ's physical resurrection from the dead. He recalls the incident of a retired pastor "who in his spare time began to study the thought of certain modern theologians." This pastor believed that their great learning was superior to his own and concluded that their views must be correct. "He understood clearly what that meant for him: His whole life and ministry had been based on a bundle of lies. He committed suicide." Dr. Craig comments, appropriately, "I believe that modern theologians must answer to God for that man's death. One cannot make statements on such matters without accepting part of the responsibility for the consequences."[88] Indeed, "We are not overstating it when we say that these are life and death issues…. If Jesus is who he claimed to be and who his followers declare him to be, then we are not dealing simply with academic questions. We are instead dealing with the most important questions of the modern person's daily life and eternal destiny."[89]

The unflattering truth about liberal theologians and other unrepentant skeptics is that they are, unfortunately, enemies of the cross of Christ and of people's hope for salvation. As the apostle Paul warned, "For, as I have often told you before and now say again even with tears, many live as enemies of the cross of Christ. Their destiny is destruction, their god is their stomach, and their glory is in their shame" (Philippians 3:18-19).

15

How unique is the Bible?

In simple chart form beginning on page 54 is concise information that readers should weigh as they consider life, their place in the universe, and what God may require of them. In asking the questions that need to be asked to find one's purpose in life, a person is inevitably drawn to the Bible, as countless millions before. And the key message of the Bible can be summed up in one sentence: "For God so loved the world that He gave His only begotten Son, that whoever believes in Him shall not perish, but have eternal life" (John 3:16 NASB). As Jesus emphasized, "This is eternal life: that they may know you, the only true God, and Jesus Christ, whom you have sent" (John 17:3). If you want to know God personally, you can begin by saying the following prayer to Him:

> Dear God: I confess my sin and turn from it. I ask Jesus Christ to enter my life and to become my Lord and Savior. I recognize this is a solemn decision that You take very seriously. I believe that on the cross Jesus Christ died for my sin, and I receive Him into my life now. My commitment to You is that I will follow Him, and I will trust You to give me the strength for this. In Jesus' name. Amen.

THE UNIQUENESS OF THE BIBLE

1. The Bible is the only book in the world that offers objective evidence to be the Word of God. Only the Bible gives real proof of its divine inspiration.

2. The Bible is the only religious Scripture in the world that is inerrant.

3. Only the Bible has unique theological content; e.g., the Bible is the only religious Scripture that offers eternal salvation as a free gift entirely by God's grace simply by believing in Jesus.

4. Only the Bible provides historic proof that the one true God sacrificially loves mankind.

5. The Bible contains the greatest moral standards of any book.

6. Only the Bible begins with the creation of the universe by divine fiat and contains a continuous, if often brief and interspersed, historical record of mankind from the first man, Adam, to the end of history.

7. Only the Bible contains detailed prophecies about the coming Savior of the world and whose prophecies have proven true in history.

8. Only the Bible has the most realistic view of human nature and the power to convict people of their sin, the ability to change human nature, and the realistic offer of a permanent solution to the problem of human sin and evil.

9. The Bible is the only ancient book with documented scientific and medical prevision. No other ancient book is ever carefully analyzed along scientific lines, but many books have been written on the theme of the Bible and modern science.

10. Only the Bible has its accuracy confirmed in history by archaeology.

11. The internal and historical characteristics of the Bible are unique in its unity and internal consistency despite production over a 1500-year period by 40-plus authors writing in several nations, discussing scores of controversial subjects yet having agreement on all issues.

12. The Bible is the most translated, purchased, memorized, and persecuted book in history.

13. Only the Bible is fully one-quarter prophetic, i.e., containing a total of some 400 complete pages of predictions.

14. Only the Bible has withstood 2000 years of intense scrutiny by critics and not only survived the attacks but prospered and had its credibility strengthened by such criticism. (Voltaire predicted the Bible would be extinct within a century; within half a century Voltaire was dead, his house a warehouse of Bibles for the Geneva Bible Society.)

15. The Bible has had more influence in the world than any other book.

16. Only the Bible has a person-specific (Christ-centered) nature for each of its 66 books detailing the person's life in prophecy, type, anti-type, etc., 400–1500 years before the person was born.

17. Only the Bible proclaims a resurrection proven in history of its central figure.

18. The Bible is the only major ancient religious Scripture whose complete textual preservation is established as virtually autographic.

Conclusion:
Learning from History

If many of the greatest persons who ever lived have made declarations such as those listed below, should not we conclude that the Bible is worthy of our personal committment to learning its teachings? Truly, the Christian church has a marvelous treasure, and presenting it to and honoring it before the world is one of its greatest privileges.

But let us ask, when was the last time you read your Bible? Have you seriously and systematically attempted to learn its teachings? Have you tried to apply these teachings in your own life?

If men and women of such caliber thought the Bible was so very important, and if it is *indeed* the Word of God Almighty, can we do anything else but apply it—and should this not become our first priority? In the end, is anything more important?

Blanche Mary Kelly was correct—the Bible is "the most stupendous book, the most sublime literature, even apart from its sacred character, in the history of the world." As was E.S. Bates: "No individual, no Caesar or Napoleon, has had such a part in the world's history as this book."

Considering the influence of the Bible, the *Encyclopedia Britannica* tells us that it has "played a special role in the history and culture of the modern world... The Bible brought its view of God, the universe, and mankind into all the leading Western languages and thus into the intellectual processes of Western man...the Bible...has been the most available, familiar, and dependable source and arbiter of intellectual, moral, and spiritual ideals in the West. Millions of modern people who do not think of themselves as religious live nevertheless with basic presuppositions that underlie biblical literature. It would be impossible to calculate the effect of such presuppositions on the changing ideas and attitudes of Western people with regard to the nature and purpose of government, social institutions, and economic theories."[90]

In *Books That Changed the World*, Robert B. Downs, former president of the American Library Association, writes:

The Bible has exercised a more profound and continuous influence upon Western civilization than has any other literary work. To consider only one phase, biblical language, style, and content pervade the writings of countless poets, dramatists, and other authors. The jurisprudence and customs of the West have been shaped by the legal and ethical precepts of the Bible. Even more fundamental, its deep insights into the motives of human nature and conduct, the tragedy of man's earthly destiny, and the search "for a better country, that is, an heavenly" have throughout the centuries directed human faith, thought, behavior, and endeavor.[91]

Eight hundred scientists of Great Britain purportedly declared the following:

We the undersigned, Students of the Natural Sciences, desire to express our sincere regret that researchers into scientific truth are perverted by some in our own times into occasion for casting doubt upon the truth and authenticity of the Holy Scriptures. We conceive that it is impossible for the Word of God written in the book of nature, and God's Word written in Holy Scripture, to contradict one another.[92]

Note what an associate chairman of the Department of Hebrew and Semitic Studies at the University of Wisconsin has to say about the Bible:

The Bible, as a religious work, needs no proof of its inspiration and authenticity. Its truth is timeless and eternally valid, one evidence of which is its continuing influence on world culture right down to the twentieth century.... Thus far, no historical statement in the Bible has ever been proved false on the basis of evidence retrieved through archeological research."[93]

Finally, consider some brief statements of the famous and influential.[94] We challenge anyone to read these short citations by some of the most significant people in history and not be impressed.

Abraham Lincoln
"This great book...is the best gift God has given to man."

Ulysses S. Grant
"To the influence of this book we are indebted for the progress made in civilization, and to this we must look as our guide in the future."

Woodrow Wilson
"A man has found himself when he has found his relation to the rest of the universe, and here is the Book in which those relations are set forth."

John Quincy Adams
"Great is my veneration for the Bible"

Sir Isaac Newton
"There are more sure marks of authenticity in the Bible than in any profane history."

Galileo
"I believe that the intention of Holy Writ was to persuade men of the truths necessary to salvation."

Cecil B. DeMille
"After more than 60 years of almost daily reading of the Bible, I never fail to find it always new and marvelously in tune with the changing needs of every day."

Johann Wolfgang von Goethe
"The Bible becomes ever more beautiful the more it is understood."

Immanuel Kant
"The Bible is the greatest benefit which the human race has ever experienced."

Charles Dickens
"The New Testament is the best book the world has ever known or will know.

Jean Jacques Rousseau
"I must confess to you that the majesty of the Scriptures astonishes me."

Isaac Newton
"I account the Scriptures of God the most sublime philosophy."

Patrick Henry
"There is a Book worth all other books which were ever printed."

William E. Gladstone
"The Bible was stamped with speciality of origin, and an immeasurable distance separates it from all competitors."

Sir William Blackstone
"The Bible has always been regarded as part of the Common Law of England."

Queen Victoria
"England has become great and happy by the knowledge of the true God through Jesus Christ.... This is the secret of England's greatness."

Mark Twain
"It is hard to make a choice of the most beautiful passage in a Book which is gemmed with beautiful passages as the Bible."

Alexander Hamilton
"I have carefully examined the evidences of the Christian religion, and if I were sitting as a juror upon its authenticity, I would unhesitatingly give my verdict in its favor."

Thomas Huxley
"The Bible has been the Magna Carta of the poor and the oppressed. The human race is not in a position to dispense with it."

Horace Greeley
"It is impossible to enslave mentally or socially a Bible-reading people. The principles of the Bible are the groundwork of human freedom."

Robert E. Lee
"In all my perplexities and distresses, the Bible has never failed to give me light and strength."

Lord Tennyson
"Bible reading is an education in itself."

Thomas Jefferson
"The studious perusal of the sacred volume will make better citizens, better fathers, and better husbands."

Samuel Taylor Coleridge
"For more than a thousand years, the Bible, collectively taken, has gone hand in hand with civilization, science, law—in short, with the moral and intellectual cultivation of the species, always supporting and leading the way."

John Locke
"The Bible is one of the greatest blessings bestowed by God on the children of man."

Roger Bacon
"I wish to show that there is one wisdom which is perfect, and that this is contained in the Scriptures."

William Lyon Phelps
"Western civilization is founded upon the Bible; all our ideas, our wisdom, our philosophy, our literature, our art, our ideals come more from the Bible than all other books put together."

RECOMMENDED READING AND WEBSITES:

Alvin J. Schmidt, *Under the Influence: How Christianity Transformed Civilization*

D. James Kennedy and Jerry Newcombe, *What if the Bible Had Never Been Written?*

Gleason Archer, *The Encyclopedia of Bible Difficulties; A Survey of Old Testament Introduction*

Mortimer Adler, *How to Read a Book*

Gordon Fee and Douglas Stuart, *How to Read the Bible for All It's Worth: A Guide to Understanding the Bible*

K.A. Kitchen, *On the Reliability of the Old Testament*

F.F. Bruce, *The New Testament Documents: Are They Reliable?*

Craig L. Blomberg, *The Historical Reliability of the Gospels*

Walter C. Kaiser, *The Old Testament Document: Are They Reliable and Relevant?*

www.johnankerberg.org

www.WalterMartin.org/links

www.WallBuilders.com

NOTES

1. Johnson's paper can be found at: <www.leaderu.com/truth/1truth08.html>.
2. Citations taken from Frank S. Meade, *The Encyclopedia of Religious Quotations*; Rhoda Tripp, *The International Thesaurus of Quotations*; Ralph L. Woods, *The World Treasury of Religious Quotations*; Jonathan Green, *Morrow's International Dictionary of Contemporary Quotations*.
3. Aldous Huxley, *Ends and Means* (London: Chatto & Windus, 1946), p. 270.
4. Original inerrancy is integrally related to both the doctrine of inspiration and the nature of God. First, the biblical doctrine of inspiration is taught to be verbal and plenary, that is, involving the very words (Matthew 4:4) and extending to every part of Scripture (2 Timothy 3:16). If God is incapable of inspiring error, whatever is inspired must be inerrant. Second, just as the Bible reveals God's nature is holy and righteous (that is, He is incapable of lying); it also reveals He is omnipotent. Because His inspiration extends to every word, it is incapable of error, and because God is omnipotent, He can safeguard the process of inspiration from error, even though it is given through fallible men. The term "the Lord says" or similar expressions are used some 2800 times in the Old Testament (Isaiah 40:8; Jeremiah 1:11; cf., Deuteronomy 18:18; 1 Kings 22:14; Amos 3:1; Exodus 34:27; Jeremiah 36:27-28; Isaiah 8:19). Inspiration (involving inerrancy) is explicitly asserted for nearly 70 percent of the Old Testament (26 of 39 books). In addition: "Twenty of twenty-two Old Testament books [or 90 percent] have their authority and/or authenticity directly affirmed by the

New Testament." (N.L. Geisler, W.E. Nix, *A General Introduction to the Bible* [Chicago: Moody Press, 1971], p. 87.) But God also preauthenticated the inspiration of the New Testament. In promising the disciples that the Holy Spirit would teach them all things and bring to remembrance the things Jesus taught them (John 14:26; referring in part to the Gospels, cf., Matthew 24:35) and that the Holy Spirit would guide them into all the truth (John 16:13-15, referring in part to the remainder of the New Testament), it is not surprising that "virtually every New Testament writer claimed that his writing was divinely authoritative…. The cumulative effect of this self-testimony is an overwhelming confirmation that the New Testament writers claimed inspiration." (Ibid., pp. 91, 97.) Some examples of New Testament claims for the inspiration include 2 Timothy 3:16; 2 Peter 1:20-21; 3:2, 15-16; Revelation 1:1-3; 22:18-19; and 1 Thessalonians 4:9.

5. Paul D. Feinberg, *The Meaning of Inerrancy* in Norman L. Geisler, ed., *Inerrancy* (Grand Rapids, MI: The Zondervan Corporation, 1979, 1980), p. 294.

6. For example, inerrancy does not require strict scientific, technical, grammatical, semantic, numeric, or historic precision. To speak of a setting sun is not error in spite of its scientific imprecision, and September 14, 15, or 16 is, properly, the middle of the month. It does not demand verbatim exactness when the New Testament quotes the Old, assuming a New Testament quotation does not contradict an Old Testament one, nor does it require any given biblical event to be exhaustively reported.

7. John Wenham, *Christ and the Bible* (Downers Grove, IL: InterVarsity, 1973), chapters 1–2, 5. See also his chapter in Geisler, ed., *Inerrancy*, pp. 3-38; Benjamin B. Warfield, *The Inspiration and Authority of the Bible*; Pierre Ch. Marcel, "Our Lord's Use of Scripture" in Henry, ed., *Revelation and the Bible* (Grand Rapids, MI: Baker, 1969), pp. 119-34 and Rene Pache, *The Inspiration and Authority of Scripture* (Chicago: Moody Press, 1966), chapter 18.

8. John Murray, "The Attestation of Scripture" in N.B. Stonehouse and Paul Woolley, eds., *The Infallible Word: A Symposium* (Grand Rapids, MI: Baker Book House, 1967, third rev. edition), pp. 26-27.

9. R.C. Sproul, "The Case for Inerrancy: A Methodological Analysis" in Montgomery, ed., *God's Inerrant Word* (Minneapolis, MN: Bethany, 1974), pp. 242-62; John Warwick Montgomery, *The Shape of the Past* (Minneapolis, MN: Bethany, 1975), pp. 138-52; Charles Feinberg in Geisler, ed., *Inerrancy*, pp. 269-87; also Warfield (above); Arthur Holmes in Geisler, ed., *Inerrancy*; and J.I. Packer, *Beyond the Battle for the Bible* (Westchester, IL: Cornerstone Books, 1980). See Geisler's comments in Geisler, ed., *Inerrancy*, p. 242, who sees some validity in each approach—inductive, deductive, adductive, and retroductive.

10. John Warwick Montgomery, *The Shape of the Past*, pp. 138-39; R.C. Sproul, "The Case of Inerrancy: A Methodological Analysis" in Montgomery, ed., *God's Inerrant Word*, p. 248, cf., 248-60.

11. John Warwick Montgomery, "Biblical Inerrancy: What Is at Stake?" in John Warwick Montgomery, ed., *God's Inerrant Word*, p. 38.

12. See <www.ronrhodes.org/Manuscript.html>.

13. Ibid.

14. Josh McDowell, *Evidence That Demands a Verdict* (San Bernardino, CA: Campus Crusade for Christ, 1969), p. 42; Robert C. Newman, "Miracles and the Historicity of the Easter Week Narratives," in Montgomery, ed., *Evidence for Faith*, pp. 281-84.

15. Geisler and Nix, *A General Introduction to the Bible*, pp. 238-39; 365-66; cf., McDowell, *Evidence That Demands a Verdict*, pp. 43-45.

16. McDowell, *Evidence That Demands a Verdict*, pp. 43-45; Clark Pinnock, *Biblical Revelation: The Foundation of Christian Theology* (Chicago: Moody Press, 1971), pp. 238-39, 365-66.

17. William M. Ramsay, *The Bearing of Recent Discovery on the Trustworthiness of the New Testament* (Grand Rapids, MI: Baker, 1959), p. 81.

18. A.N. Sherwin-White, *Roman Society and Roman Law in the New Testament* (Oxford: Clarendon Press, 1963) from Norman L. Geisler, *Christian Apologetics* (Grand Rapids, MI: Baker, 1976), p. 326.

19. McDowell, *Evidence That Demands a Verdict*, rev. 1979, pp. 39-52; Geisler and Nix, *A General Introduction to the Bible*, pp. 238, 357-67.

20. Gary Habermas, *Ancient Evidence for the Life of Jesus* (Nashville, TN: Thomas Nelson, 1973), pp.112-15; cf., F.F. Bruce, *The New Testament Documents: Are They Reliable?* (Downers Grove, IL: InterVarsity, 1971), chapters 9-10.

21. John Wenham, *Redating Matthew, Mark and Luke* (Downers Grove, IL: InterVarsity, 1992), pp. 115-19, 136, 183, see pp. xxv, 147, 198, 200, 221, 223, 238-39, 243-5.

22. John A.T. Robinson, *Redating the New Testament* (Philadelphia: Westminster, 1976).

23. Cf. Wenham, *Redating Matthew, Mark and Luke*, p. 200.

24. F.F. Bruce, "Are the New Testament Documents Still Reliable?" in *Christianity Today* (October 28, 1978), p. 33.

25. E.g., Gerhard Meier, *The End of the Historical Critical Method* (St. Louis, MO: Concordia, 1977) and Josh McDowell, *More Evidence That Demands a Verdict* (San Bernardino, CA: Campus Crusade for Christ, 1972).

26. For examples, see our *Fast Facts on Defending Your Faith* (Eugene, OR: Harvest House, 2002), pp. 136-48.

27. See J.W. Montgomery, *The Law Above the Law* (Minneapolis, MN: Bethany, 1975), appendix reproducing this work, pp. 91-140.

28. Reproduced in *The Simon Greenleaf Law Review*, vol. 1 (Orange, CA: The Faculty of the Simon Greenleaf School of Law, 1981–1982), pp. 15-74.

29. Irwin Linton, *A Lawyer Examines the Bible* (San Diego: Creation-Life-Publishers, 1977), p. 45.

30. Montgomery, *The Law Above the Law*, pp. 87-88.

31. Norman Geisler, *Christ: The Theme of the Bible* (Chicago: Moody Press, 1969), 29n citing D.J. Wiseman, "Archaeological Confirmations of the Old Testament in Carl F. Henry, ed., *Revelation and the Bible* (Grand Rapids, MI: Baker, 1958), pp. 301-02.

32. Clifford Wilson, *Archaeology, the Bible and Christ* (Pacific Christian Ministries, P.O. Box 311, Lilydale 3140, Victoria, Australia), vol. 17, p. 62; available in the U.S. from Pacific International University and Archaeology Center, P.O. Box 1717, Springfield, Missouri 65801 (417-831-7515).

33. E.M. Blaiklock, "Editor's Preface," *The New International Dictionary of Biblical Archaeology* (Grand Rapids, MI: Regency Reference Library/Zondervan, 1983), pp. vii-viii, emphasis added.

34. J.A. Thompson, *The Bible and Archaeology* (Grand Rapids, MI: Eerdmans, 1975), p. 5.

35. Norman Geisler and Ron Brooks, *When Skeptics Ask: A Handbook on Christian Evidences* (Wheaton, IL: Victor, 1990), p. 200.

36. Ibid.

37. John Warwick Montgomery, "The Jury Returns: A Juridicial Defense of Christianity" in Montgomery, ed., *Evidence for Faith: Deciding the God Question* (Dallas: Word, 1991), p. 326.

38. John Elder, *Prophets, Idols and Diggers* (NY: Bobbs Merrill, 1960), p. 16, from Gleason L. Archer Jr., *A Survey of Old Testament Introduction* (Chicago, IL: Moody Press, 1974), rev., p. 166.

39. W.F. Albright, *The Archaeology of Palestine*, rev. (Pelican books, 1960), p. 127.

40. Keith N. Schoville, *Biblical Archaeology in Focus* (Grand Rapids, MI: Baker, 1978), p. 163; cf., Geisler and Brooks, *When Skeptics Ask*, p. 179.

41. A.H. Sayce, *Monument Facts and Higher Critical Fancies* (London: The Religious Tract Society, 1904), p. 23, cited in Josh McDowell, *More Evidence That Demands a Verdict*, p. 53.

42. As cited in McDowell, *Evidence That Demands a Verdict*, p. 66.

43. E.M. Blaiklock, *Christianity Today*, September 28, 1973, p. 13.

44. E.g., Edwin Yamauchi, *The Stone and the Scriptures* (NY: J.B. Lippencott, 1972), pp. 30,161.

45. Joseph P. Free, revised and expanded by Howard F. Vos, *Archaeology and Bible History* (Grand Rapids: Zondervan, 1992), pp. 255-57.

46. Cf. Craig L. Blomberg, "Where Do We Start Studying Jesus?" in Michael J. Wilkins and J.P. Moreland, eds., *Jesus Under Fire: Modern Scholarship Reinvents the Historical Jesus* (Grand Rapids, MI: Zondervan 1995), p. 221.

47. W. Arndt, *Does the Bible Contradict Itself: A Discussion of Alleged Contradictions in the Bible* (St. Louis, MO: Concordia, 5th ed. rev. 1955); John W. Haley, *Alleged Discrepancies of the Bible* (Grand Rapids, MI: Baker, rpt. 1982); Gleason Archer, *The Encyclopedia of Bible Difficulties* (Grand Rapids, MI: Zondervan, 1982).

48. E.g., Gleason Archer, *A Survey of Old Testament Introduction* (Chicago, IL: Moody Press, 1974, rev.); Josh McDowell, *Daniel in the Critic's Den* (San Bernardino, CA: Campus Crusade for Christ, 1973); R.D. Wilson, *Studies in the Book of Daniel*, two vols. rpt. (Grand Rapids, MI: Baker, 1979); see "Bible Criticism," in Norman Geisler, *Baker Encyclopedia of Christian Apologetics* (Grand Rapids, MI: Baker, 1999).

49. K.A. Kitchen, *Ancient Orient and Old Testament* (Chicago: InterVarsity Press, 1973), p. 23, first emphasis added.

50. John Warwick Montgomery, *The Shape of the Past*, p. 176.

51. Gleason Archer, *Encyclopedia of Bible Difficulties*, pp. 11-12.

52. R. D. Wilson, *Scientific Investigation of the Old Testament* (Chicago: Moody, 1959), pp. 13, 20, 130,162-63; David Otis Fuller, ed., *Which Bible?* (Grand Rapids, MI: Grand Rapids International Publications, rev. 1971, 2nd edition), p. 44.

53. William Arndt, *Does the Bible Contradict Itself?* (St. Louis: Concordia, 1955, rpt.), p. XI.

54. J. Barton Payne, *Encyclopedia of Biblical Prophecy: The Complete Guide to Scriptural Predictions and Their Fulfillment* (New York: Harper & Row, 1973), p.13.

55. John Wesley White, *Re-Entry* (Grand Rapids, MI: Zondervan, 1971), p. 14; cf. ibid., p. 680.

56. See John MacArthur, *The Second Coming: Signs of Christ's Return and the End of the Age* (Wheaton, IL: Crossway, 2003).

57. Gleason Archer Jr., *A Survey of Old Testament Introduction*, pp. 326-51.

58. See Josh McDowell, *Daniel in the Critics' Den*; John Walvoord, *Daniel: the Key to Prophetic Revelation* (Chicago: Moody, 1972).

59. Adapted from Norman Geisler, Ron Brooks, *When Skeptics Ask: A Handbook of Christian Evidences* (Wheaton, IL: Victor Books, 1990), pp. 114-15.

60. A good place to start is Os Guiness, *God in the Dark: The Assurance of Faith Beyond a Shadow of Doubt* (Wheaton, IL: Crossway, 1996).

61. Mark Eastman, Chuck Missler, *The Creator Beyond Time and Space* (Costa Mesa, CA: The Word for Today, 1996), p. 23.

62. Ibid., p. 87.

63. Ibid., p. 101.

64. A.E. Wilder-Smith, *The Reliability of the Bible* (San Diego: Master Books, 1983), p. 39.

65. Eastman and Missler, *The Creator Beyond Time and Space*, p. 101.

66. James Smith, *What the Bible Teaches About the Promised Messiah* (Nashville, TN: Nelson, 1993); J. Barton Payne, *Encyclopedia of Biblical Prophecy*; Alfred Edersheim, *The Life and Times of Jesus the Messiah* (Grand Rapids, MI: Eerdmans, 1972).

67. Peter W. Stoner, *Science Speaks: Scientific Proof of the Accuracy of Prophecy and the Bible* (Chicago: Moody Press, 1969), p. 4.

68. Ibid., p. 109.

69. Adapted from James Coppedge, *Evolution: Possible or Impossible?* (Grand Rapids, MI: Zondervan, 1973), p. 120.

70. Emile Borel, *Probabilities and Life* (New York: Dover, 1962), chapters 1 and 3; Borel's cosmic limit of 10^{200} changes nothing in this calculation. See the improvement in Borel's law, Dembski's "Law of Small Probability"—"Specified events of small probability do not occur by chance"—in William A. Dembski, *The Design Inference* (New York: Cambridge University Press, 1998), pp. 2-9. "In eliminating chance, the design inference eliminates not just a single chance hypothesis, but all relevant chance hypotheses" (p. 8).

71. J.P. Moreland, ed., *The Creation Hypothesis: Scientific Evidence for an Intelligent Designer* (Downer's Grove, IL: InterVarsity Press, 1994); Michael Wilkins and J.P. Moreland, *Jesus Under Fire: Modern Scholarship Reinvents the Historical Jesus* (Downer's Grove, IL: InterVarsity, 1995).

72. James Still, "Critique of New Testament Reliability and 'Bias' in NT Development" at: <www.infidels.org>.

73. See Walter Maier, *Form Criticism Reexamined* (St. Louis, MO: Concordia Publishing House, 1973), pp. 7-10.

74. Ibid., p. 38.

75. Ankerberg and Weldon, *Fast Facts on Defending Your Faith*, pp. 131-36.

76. Robert W. Funk, Roy W. Hoover, and the Jesus Seminar, *The Five Gospels: The Search for the Authentic Words of Jesus* (New York: MacMillan, 1993), p. 5.

77. Ibid., p. 16.

78. Ibid., p. 19.

79. Ibid, p. 2.

80. Ibid., pp. 5, 35.

81. Craig Blomberg, "The Seventy-Four 'Scholars': Who Does the Jesus Seminar Really Speak For?" in *Christian Research Journal*, Fall 1994, p. 29.

82. John Wenham, *Redating Matthew, Mark and Luke* (Downer's Grove, IL: InterVarsity, 1992), p. 3.

83. Charlotte Allen, "The Search for a No-Frills Jesus," *The Atlantic Monthly*, December 1996, p. 67.

84. Ibid, p. 56.

85. Wenham, *Redating Matthew, Mark and Luke*, p. 42.

86. Gregory A. Boyd, *Cynic, Sage or Son of God?* (Wheaton, IL: Bridge Point, 1995), p. 142.

87. Ibid., p. 142.

88. William Lane Craig, *The Son Rises* (Chicago: Moody Press, 1981), pp. 135-36.

89. Michael J. Wilkins and J.P. Moreland, "Introduction: The Furor Surrounding Jesus," in Wilkins and Moreland, *Jesus Under Fire*, pp. 6, 11.

90. *Encyclopedia Britannica*, Macropaedia, Vol. 2, p. 880.

91. Robert B. Downs, *Books That Changed the World* (NY: New American Library/Mentor, rev., 1983), p. 40.

92. http://logosresourcepages.org/quotes.html cited by Pastor David L. Brown, Ph.D., First Baptist Church, Oak Creek, Wisconsin. The Creation Research Society with hundreds of scientists has as part of its Statement of Belief: "The *Bible* is the written Word of God, and because it is inspired throughout, all its assertions are historically and scientifically true in the original autographs." http://www.creationresearch.org/about_crs.htm.

93. Keith N. Schoville, *Biblical Archaeology in Focus* (Grand Rapids, MI: Baker, 1978), p. 156.

94. Taken from a variety of famous/contemporary quotation volumes. Statements at http://logosresourcepages.org/quotes.html were compiled by Pastor David L. Brown, Ph.D., First Baptist Church, Oak Creek, Wisconsin.

Karen's
School Picture

**Here are some other books
about Karen
that you might enjoy:**

Karen's Witch

Karen's Roller Skates

Karen's Worst Day

Karen's Kittycat Club

Karen's
School Picture

ANN M. MARTIN

Illustrations by Susan Tang

A
LITTLE
APPLE
PAPERBACK

SCHOLASTIC INC.

New York Toronto London Auckland Sydney
Mexico City New Delhi Hong Kong Buenos Aires

#5

ISBN 0-439-37964-4

12 11 10 9 8 7 6 5 4 3 2 1   2 3 4 5 6 7/0

Printed in the U.S.A.   40

First printing of this revised edition, February 2002

This book is for
Ashley Vinsel

School Pictures

"Hi, Ms. Colman! Hi, Ms. Colman!" I cried.

Ms. Colman is my second-grade teacher. She is very, very, very nice. She always helps kids and never yells at them. So I like her a lot.

Some kids don't like school, but I do. I like school on Monday mornings. I even like school when it gives me a headache or makes my eyes hurt. School can do that to you, you know.

I am Karen Brewer. I am six years old. I

am only supposed to be in first grade, but after I started first grade, my teacher said, "Karen can do second-grade work. Let's put her in second grade." So Mommy and Daddy said okay, and the next thing I knew, I was in Ms. Colman's class.

That was fine with me. My two best friends are Hannie Papadakis and Nancy Dawes. They were already in Ms. Colman's class. They sat in the back row. Ms. Colman said I could sit next to them if the three of us promised to pay attention. We are pretty good about paying attention, but sometimes I have to let Nancy smell my strawberry eraser or something. Then Ms. Colman just says, "Back to work, girls."

There are sixteen kids in my class. We sit at desks in rows — four rows of four desks. The fourth person in my row is Ricky Torres. He is a pest. Luckily he sits at one end of the row and I sit at the other end. Hannie is the one who got stuck sitting next to him.

"Good morning, Karen," my teacher replied.

It was a Monday morning and I bounced into our classroom. Another week of school was about to begin. Another week of worksheets and gym and stories.

Ms. Colman smiled at me and I smiled back.

I ran to my desk and checked on my strawberry eraser. There it was. Then I hung my coat on my hook in the coat room. When I came out I saw Hannie and Nancy.

"Hi! Hi, you guys!" I cried.

Nancy lives next door to me and sometimes we ride to school together, but not that morning.

"Look what I got," said Hannie. She held out a purse shaped like a cat. Hannie and I like cats a lot.

"Aw, how adorable. How cuuuuuute," said a voice.

Hannie and Nancy and I looked up. It was Ricky Torres.

"Be quiet, Yicky Ricky," I said.

Ricky opened his mouth to say something mean back to me. Before he could, Ms.

Colman clapped her hands. "Time to get ready for attendance," she announced.

Another day of school had begun.

Guess what. It turned out not to be just *any* old day. At the very end, Ms. Colman said, "Class, I have a special announcement. In two weeks, it will be school-picture day. Each of you will have your own picture taken, and then we will have our class picture taken. All of us together."

4

"Oh, goody!" I couldn't help exclaiming.

I just *love* having my picture taken. I love to get dressed up. I love to tie a ribbon in my hair. School-picture day would be very wonderful.

I was so excited that I ignored Yicky Ricky when he said in a high, silly voice, "Oh, goody!" just like I had done.

I didn't even pay attention to the headache I had. Or to my eyes, which were hurting again. All I could think about was what I would wear the day our pictures were taken.

"Let's stand together in the class picture," I whispered to Nancy.

"Yeah!" she replied. She passed the message on to Hannie.

Hannie grinned at me.

What a great day it had been! How could I wait two whole weeks to have my picture taken?

Two Families

"Mommy! Hey, Mommy! In two weeks it will be school-picture day!" I called.

Nancy and I ran out of Stoneybrook Academy. That is the private school we go to. Hannie's brother Linny goes there, too, and someday her baby sister Sari and my little brother Andrew will go there. Nancy doesn't have any brothers or sisters.

"School-picture day," said Mommy. "I can tell you are very excited."

"Yes," I said, as Nancy and I climbed in the car. "I can't wait to get all those little pictures. The ones you can cut up and give to special people after you write, 'Love, Karen' on the backs."

"Am I a special person?" spoke up Andrew, who was sitting in the front seat next to Mommy. Andrew is four.

"Of course you are," I replied. Then I added grandly, "You can have two pictures if there are enough."

I settled back against the seat while Mommy

drove Nancy and Andrew and me home. My head hurt. I rubbed my eyes.

I saw Mommy glancing at me in the rearview mirror.

"I have a headache," I told her. "Another one."

"We worked very hard in school today," Nancy told my mother.

"And you are a busy girl, Karen," added Mommy. "You have homework now, and meetings of the Fun Club."

I nodded. My headaches always went away after I'd been home for awhile.

"Karen?" said Andrew, turning around to look at me. "Are you going to give pictures to everyone in the little house and everyone in the big house?"

"Yup," I replied.

The people in the little house are Mommy and Andrew and Seth and me. Seth is my stepfather. His last name is Engle, so Mommy's last name is Engle now, too. But Andrew and I are still Brewers, like Daddy. Also at the little house are Midgie and

8

Rocky, but they are a dog and a cat. I will not need to give them pictures.

The people at the big house are Daddy and Elizabeth and Charlie and Sam and Kristy and David Michael and Emily Michelle and Nannie. And Andrew and me when we visit them. Oh, and Shannon and Boo-Boo. They are another dog and cat. They won't need pictures, either. Even so, I wonder if I will have enough pictures for my friends *and* for everyone in my two families.

That's what the big house and the little house are. The places where my two families live. A long time ago, Mommy and Daddy got divorced. Then they each got married again. Elizabeth is Daddy's wife. She's my stepmother. And Charlie, Sam, Kristy, and David Michael are Elizabeth's kids. They're my stepbrothers and stepsister. Emily Michelle is my adopted sister. Daddy and Elizabeth adopted her. She came all the way from a country called Vietnam. She is only two years old. And Nannie is Elizabeth's mother, so she is sort of my grandmother.

I call myself Karen Two-Two. I call my brother Andrew Two-Two. That's because once Ms. Colman read our class a book called *Jacob Two-Two Meets the Hooded Fang*. I think the name Karen Two-Two is just right for me since I have two of everything. I have two houses. I have two families (one at each house). I have two dogs (one at each house) and two cats (one at each house). In fact, I have lots of twos that are one at each house — a stuffed cat named Goosie at the little house and a stuffed cat named Moosie at the big house, clothes at the little house and clothes at the big house, toys at the little house and toys at the big house. Andrew does, too. We live at the big house every other weekend, so when we go there, we don't have to remember to take a lot of things with us.

It might sound like fun being a two-two, and usually it is. But sometimes it isn't. For instance, I only had one special blanket, Tickly, and I had to rip Tickly in half so that

I could have a piece at the big house and a piece at the little house. I didn't mind too much, though. I just said, "Ouch," for Tickly and then it was over.

As we drove home from school that day, I closed my eyes to make them stop hurting.

I practiced a movie-star smile. I forgot about my eyes and about being a two-two, and thought of school pictures instead.

Karen's Turn to Read

Friday, Friday, Friday! Every other Friday, Andrew and I get ready to leave the little house and stay with Daddy and our big-house family for the weekend.

Mommy drives us over. Andrew and I are always very excited. I was so excited that my aching eyes didn't bother me. We don't usually do anything very special at the big house. I just like being with my other family.

Maybe I better tell you about the people in my other family, since there are so many of them. The big house sounds confusing, but it isn't.

First there are Daddy and Elizabeth. They are the parents. They are also stepparents to each other's kids. Elizabeth is a very nice stepmother to Andrew and me. And I think that Daddy is a nice stepfather to Kristy and her brothers.

Charlie and Sam are Elizabeth's two oldest kids. They are so old they are in high school.

Then there is Kristy. She is thirteen. She is one of my favorite, favorite people in the big house or anywhere. Kristy does a lot of baby-sitting. She even has a business called the Baby-sitters Club. Sometimes she sits for Andrew and David Michael and Emily and me.

David Michael is my eight-year-old stepbrother. Mostly he is a pain like Ricky Torres. But at least he collects bugs, so that's okay.

Emily Michelle is the youngest person at the big house. Before Daddy and Elizabeth adopted her, Andrew was the youngest

person. And I was the youngest girl. Sometimes I am not sure how I feel about Emily.
She's too little to play with — but she's
awfully cute. I feel like I don't know her
very well, though.

After Emily moved in, so did Nannie.
Nannie is Kristy's favorite grandmother.
She takes care of Emily when Daddy and
Elizabeth are at work and everyone else is
at school.

And then, of course, there are Shannon
and Boo-Boo. The big house is very full and
busy. When Andrew and I are visiting, ten
people and two pets live there. That is one
reason I like the big house so much. There
is always something going on.

Most nights, I do not like to go to bed. I
would rather stay up. I do not want to miss
out on anything. But when Daddy says,
"Bedtime, Karen," he means bedtime.

Kristy always makes bedtime easier. When
my nightgown is on and I am under the
covers with Moosie and Tickly, Kristy comes

14

into my room. She always says, "What book shall we read tonight?"

For the longest time, I would answer, "*The Witch Next Door*," since I think Mrs. Porter, our next-door neighbor, is a witch. Now Kristy and I read chapter books. We had finished *Charlotte's Web*. So I said, "How about starting *Mrs. Piggle-Wiggle*?"

"Fine," replied Kristy. She found the book on my shelf. She brought it to my bed. Then she climbed onto my bed and sat next to

me. "Do you want to read first?" she asked. (Kristy and I take turns reading.)

"Okay," I said.

I read the first page.

I read the second page.

I was supposed to read four more pages, until I got to the middle of the first chapter. Then Kristy would finish the chapter. But my eyes were hurting again.

"Kristy," I said, after page two, "I can't read anymore. My eyes hurt. So does my head."

"You must be tired," said Kristy. "You've had a long week. I'll finish the chapter for you. Maybe," she added, "you should slow down a little. You do an awful lot for someone who is six."

"Almost seven," I reminded her.

"Even so."

Kristy did finish the chapter. It was very funny. By the time she was done, my headache was gone.

Karen's Headache

Blechhh.

I like Saturdays. I like *any* Saturday. But a sunny Saturday is better than a rainy Saturday. And when I woke up the next morning, I found a rainy Saturday. I found a dreary, gray, wet, blechhh day.

But do you know what Daddy said that morning after breakfast? He said, "Today is a perfect day."

"Perfect for what?" replied Sam. "Ducks?"

I giggled.

"No," said Daddy. "Perfect for building

a fire in the fireplace and reading aloud. That would be very cozy."

Usually Sam and Charlie go off on the weekends. They do grown-up things with their high-school friends. But that day they didn't have any plans. They did not seem very excited about reading aloud by the fire, but they couldn't think of anything else to do.

So in a little while, my whole big-house family was sitting in the living room. Daddy had made a roaring fire. It was crackling and popping. It shot orange sparks up the chimney.

Shannon and Boo-Boo lay down on the rug in front of the fireplace. Daddy and Elizabeth sat on the couch. Elizabeth held Emily in her lap. I sat in Kristy's lap in an armchair. Nannie sat in another armchair. And all the boys — Andrew, David Michael, Sam, and Charlie — sat around on the floor.

"What are we going to read?" I asked.

"We are going to start a book called *Mrs*.

Frisby and the Rats of NIMH," replied Daddy.

"I know that story!" cried Andrew.

"Yes," said Daddy, "but you have only seen it on a video cassette. The story in the book is a little different."

"It's longer," said David Michael.

"But I think you will like it," spoke up Elizabeth. "It's a story that both grown-ups and children can enjoy."

"We'll take turns reading," said Daddy. "I'll start. Then anyone who wants to can take a turn."

So Daddy put on his reading glasses. He began the story about Mrs. Frisby, the mother mouse, who has to move her children and her house before the farmer with the big plow comes and runs over them. Elizabeth was right. Even Sam and Charlie were interested in the story. It was not a baby book.

After Daddy read for awhile, Elizabeth took a turn. Then Charlie, and then Kristy.

When Kristy was finished, she said, "Karen

do you want a turn? Some of these words are hard, but you're a very good reader."

"Okay," I said. But after about half a page, my head hurt again.

"This story is too hard," I said. "I give up my turn."

"Karen, you were doing just fine," Kristy told me. "I know the print is small, but you read every word perfectly." She paused. After a moment she said, "Hey, last night you got a headache reading *Mrs. Piggle-Wiggle* and gave up your turn then, too. What's going on?"

"Try reading again," Daddy suggested to me. "Hold the book closer."

I tried. The words swam before my eyes. I held the book farther away. That wasn't any better.

"Hmm," said Daddy. "It seems to me that your work in school has not been as good as usual lately. I think maybe you need to see an ophthalmologist."

"A what?" I asked.

"An eye doctor."

20

"An eye doctor! You mean to get *glasses?* No way. I don't want glasses!"

"Well, you may need them. After all, your mom wears glasses. And I wear glasses for reading. It makes sense."

I didn't say another word. But I was *not* going to get glasses.

Rocky's Tail

Usually, when Mommy picks Andrew and me up at Daddy's on Sunday night, she just pulls the car into the drive and honks. Then Andrew and I say good-bye to everyone at the big house and run out to the car.

But tonight, Daddy walked out to the car with us. "Listen," he said to Mommy, "I need to talk to you. I think Karen needs to see an eye doctor. She's been getting lots of headaches."

"That's true," said Mommy.

"And her schoolwork hasn't been as good as usual lately."

"I know."

"And this weekend, we realized that every time Karen has to read something, especially if the print is small, she gets a headache. Or she squints her eyes. Or she holds the book closer or farther away."

"I'll make an appointment with Doctor Gourson tomorrow," said Mommy.

"Nooooo!" I howled.

"She doesn't want glasses," Daddy said to Mommy. He whispered, but I heard him anyway.

"Of course I don't!" I exclaimed. "They'll make me look funny."

"But think how much better you'll feel," said Mommy.

"No glasses," I said flatly, as we drove away.

"We'll see," replied Mommy.

The next day, Mrs. Dawes, Nancy's

mother, drove Nancy and me home from
school. As usual, my head ached and my
eyes hurt. But when I walked into our
kitchen, I said, "Hi, Mommy! Guess what.
My head doesn't hurt at all. My eyes do
not hurt, either. I think I just had a virus.
Maybe I had the flu or a very bad head
cold."

Mommy smiled at me. "I'm glad you're
feeling better," she said.

"I think I will fix a snack," I said. "Maybe
Andrew would like one, too. Andrew!" I
called.

"What?" he answered. He ran into the
kitchen.

"Would you like a snack?" I asked him.
"I will fix us Oreo cookies and milk."

"Sure!" said Andrew.

I am always starving when I get home
from school. I need food right away. "You
get the cookies, I'll get the milk and the
glasses," I told Andrew.

Andrew put the package of cookies on

the kitchen table. I set out two glasses. Then I carried the big carton of milk to the table. I opened it and began to pour.

SPLOOSH!

"Karen! Look at what you're doing!" cried Mommy, jumping up.

I looked. I was pouring milk . . . wasn't I?

"Karen, stop!" exclaimed Andrew.

I stopped. I looked at the table. I leaned over and looked more closely. I had poured

the milk, but I had missed the glass. The milk was all over the table. It was running onto the floor.

I couldn't help it. I began to cry.

"I'm sorry!" I said. I ran out of the kitchen.

"Look out, Karen!" I heard Andrew shout from behind me.

Too late. I tripped over Rocky and stepped on his tail. I hadn't even seen him.

"MROW!" cried Rocky angrily. He turned around and began licking his tail.

I couldn't blame him for being mad. I flopped on the couch in the living room and cried and cried. Soon I felt someone sit down next to me. Then Mommy's voice said, "Don't worry, honey. I called Doctor Gourson today. I made an appointment for you to see him on Thursday."

I nodded miserably. I didn't want glasses. Not at all. But I felt terrible about Rocky. And besides, my head really did hurt. So did my eyes.

6

The Ophthalmologist

The only good thing about going to Dr. Gourson was that my appointment was at twelve-thirty in the afternoon. I got to miss over two hours of school. Even though I like school, a little vacation is always nice. I felt very important when Ms. Colman looked at her watch and said it was time to go meet Mommy. Everyone else was stuck working on subtraction problems. I got to put on my jacket and leave. I knew my classmates were watching me and wishing they could leave, too.

Mommy and I had to sit for a very long time in the waiting room at Dr. Gourson's office. I never understand that. How come doctors always tell you to come so early? It is a gigundo waste of time.

"Mommy, I'm bored," I said. I wished Andrew were there, but he was staying with Mrs. Dawes while we were at Dr. Gourson's.

Mommy gave me a pad of paper and a pencil. "Why don't you draw some pictures?" she suggested.

I drew a picture of everyone in my two families. Then I put glasses on each person. Except me.

A nurse came to the doorway of the waiting room. "Karen Brewer?" he said.

Mommy and I stood up. We followed the nurse into a dim room. Lots and lots of machines and equipment were in it.

"Have a seat right here," said the nurse. Then he left.

I climbed into a big chair. It was like a dentist's chair.

Mommy sat on a regular chair nearby.

Dr. Gourson made us wait a while longer. At last he came in.

"Hi," he said. "I'm Doctor Gourson. You must be Karen."

I nodded.

Mommy and Dr. Gourson already knew each other. They said hello. Then they talked about me and my eyes. Finally, Dr. Gourson pointed to a chart on the wall across the room. At the top of the chart were some big E's. They looked like this:

E ꞟ ꭟ Ш

"Show me which way the E's are pointing," said the doctor.

So I did. That was easy. See? I didn't need glasses after all.

Next Dr. Gourson said, "Karen, how old are you?"

"Six," I replied.

"And do you know the letters in the alphabet?" he asked.

"Of course I do. Mommy told you I can read," I said to him. What a silly question.

"Karen," said Mommy warningly.

"Sorry," I told the doctor.

"That's quite all right," he replied. "Then start with the top row of letters and read down as far as you can."

I began reading. I read one row. Two rows. By the third row, the letters were a big blur.

"I can't read anymore," I had to tell Dr. Gourson. "But it isn't because I *can't read*. It's just that I can't see those little letters from way back here."

"Okay," replied the doctor. Then he did a whole lot of other things with my eyes.

First he put drops in them. The drops made my eyes run.

Then he looked at my eyes through all sorts of instruments. I didn't have to do anything but sit there, or, sometimes roll my eyes around, while he looked.

At last he said, "Karen? Mrs. Engle? You may go back to the waiting room now."

31

(The waiting room? Again?) "The nurse will call you in a little while and we can talk about Karen's eyes."

Oh, goody. Hurray. Just what I wanted.

The waiting room was even more boring this time than before. That was because those drops had made my eyes so blurry that I could hardly see. I couldn't read or draw pictures or do anything.

So Mommy read to me while we waited.

Karen's Glasses

"Karen Brewer?" said the nurse again.

Mommy and I stood up, and Mommy followed the nurse back to Dr. Gourson's office. She had to lead me by the hand. I could not see where I was going.

Dr. Gourson was sitting behind a desk in his office. Mommy and I sat on the other side of the desk. I sat in Mommy's lap.

"Well, Karen does need glasses," Dr. Gourson began. "She needs them pretty badly."

"Just for reading?" I asked hopefully. "Like Daddy and Seth?"

"No, I'm afraid not. You'll need them for reading and for all the time. In fact, you'll need two pairs of glasses."

"Two pairs!" I exclaimed. What would I do with two pairs of glasses?

"Yes," said the doctor. "You'll need one pair of glasses to help you see clearly when you're reading or doing other things up close. You'll need a second pair to help you see clearly the rest of the time."

I couldn't believe it. Glasses. I would never look like a movie star if I had to wear glasses. I almost began to cry, but I stopped myself.

Dr. Gourson gave Mommy a slip of paper. "These are the prescriptions for Karen's lenses," he told her. "There's an optometrist right here in the building, and — "

"What's an optometrist?" I interrupted.

"He's a person who makes glasses," said Dr. Gourson. "You can choose the frames you like. Then the optometrist will put the

34

right lenses into them so that you'll be able to see."

Mommy and I left Dr. Gourson's office. We walked down a hallway. Mommy opened a door with some blurry letters on it. We went inside and she stepped up to a desk. A woman was standing behind the desk.

"Hello," Mommy said to the woman. "I am Mrs. Engle. This is my daughter, Karen. We have just come from Doctor Gourson's office. Karen needs two pairs of glasses." She handed the woman the slip of paper.

The woman looked at me and smiled. "Two pairs of glasses for Karen Engle," she said.

"Brewer," I corrected her. (That is another problem with being a two-two.)

Mommy explained about our names. Then the woman gave the prescription to the optometrist. When she came back, she said, "Let's look at frames. What kind of glasses do you want, Karen?"

"No glasses," I told her.

"*Karen*," said Mommy.

"Sorry," I said. "Um, I don't know what kind of glasses I want."

"Well, I'll show you some things. You will probably want different frames so that you can tell your reading glasses from your other glasses."

"Okay," I said.

"Come sit here," said the woman. She led me to a counter and lifted me onto a stool. My eyes were starting to clear up from the drops. I could see racks and racks of glasses frames on the counter. In front of me was a big mirror.

I tried on lots of glasses. I tried on white ones. I tried on round tan ones like Mommy's and square brown ones like Daddy's and gold-rimmed ones like Seth's.

"Yuck," I said about each pair.

Then the woman showed me a pair of pink glasses.

"Pink!" I exclaimed. "I can get *pink* glasses?!"

"They come in blue, too," said the woman. "A nice pale blue."

36

"I'll take them!" I said.

Mommy and the lady smiled.

When the optometrist had put the lenses in my glasses, Mommy and I walked out to the car. I put on my pink glasses. My blue glasses were going to be the ones for reading.

"I cannot believe it!" I cried. "Everything looks so much clearer. Brighter, too."

I knew I would never be a movie star now, but it was nice to see clearly again.

Glasses Everywhere!

Mommy and I got home just after school let out. I spent most of the afternoon trying on my two pairs of glasses and looking at myself in the mirror.

"I do not look so bad," I said to Goosie. Goosie was in the bathroom with me. I held him up to the mirror. "See? I do not look bad at all. I still look pretty much like Karen Brewer — wearing glasses."

Before I left school that day, Ms. Colman had given me my homework. I took it into the kitchen when Mommy began making dinner.

Mommy stood at the kitchen counter, reading a recipe. She was wearing her tan glasses.

I sat at the table with my workbook. I was wearing my blue glasses. (The words in the workbook were nice and clear.)

I thought of Seth and Daddy at work. They were probably wearing their glasses.

When Andrew came into the kitchen with his fire truck, I realized something.

"Hey, Andrew!" I exclaimed. "You're the only person at the little house who *doesn't* wear glasses. There are glasses everywhere!"

"So?" said Andrew. He sounded cross.

"Don't be mad," I told him. "It's okay if you don't need glasses. Hey, Mommy, this workbook page is really easy. I can read every single word."

"Good," said Mommy. "That sounds like my old Karen."

I finished my workbook pages in record

time. Mommy checked them. I had answered every question right!

I put my workbook away. Then I took off my blue glasses and put on my pink ones. I looked at myself in the bathroom mirror again. This time I tried out my movie-star smile. Even with glasses it looked okay.

"Mommy!" I called. "Can I go over to Nancy's and show her my glasses?"

"Yes," she replied. "But be home in half an hour. It's almost dinnertime."

"Okay!"

I ran out our front door, across our lawn, across Nancy's driveway, and along the walk to *her* front door. I was still wearing my pink glasses. I was carrying the blue ones in a case that the optometrist had given Mommy and me for free.

Ding-dong!

Nancy answered the door.

"Hi, Karen!" she cried. "Oh, you got them!"

I nodded. "Do you like them?"

"You know what? You don't look that different."

"I don't?"

"Nope."

That was good to know. "But do you like them?" I asked again.

"Sure," replied Nancy. "They're neat."

"Can I come in? I'll show you the other pair. I had to get *two* pairs."

Nancy let me inside. I modeled the blue glasses for her. Then I modeled both pairs of glasses for her mother. Then her father came home. I modeled them for him, too.

Mrs. Dawes said I looked lovely.

Mr. Dawes said I looked dashing.

I went home. I modeled my glasses for Seth. He said I looked grown up.

I was feeling a lot better about wearing glasses.

That night, I tried the pink glasses on Goosie. I tried the blue ones on my stuffed elephant. Then I took them off and put them on two of my dolls.

"Hey, Andrew!" I called. "Come here."

Andrew came into my room. He looked at the dolls. "See?" he said as I took the glasses off the dolls. "I am not the only one around here who does not wear glasses."

We laughed. "Rocky and Midgie don't wear them, either," I pointed out.

When Andrew left, I looked through the clothes in my closet. I decided that the next day I would wear my jeans and my unicorn shirt to school. The shirt is pink and blue with a white satin unicorn on the front. No matter which pair of glasses I wore, they would match my outfit. I would not look like a movie star, but I would look lovely and dashing and grown up.

I was ready for school.

Yicky Ricky

The next morning, I woke up with a funny feeling in my stomach.

"Mommy?" I said, when I went into the kitchen for breakfast. "I don't feel too good. My stomach feels jumpy."

"Does it hurt?" she asked. She put her hand on my forehead to see if I had a fever.

"No," I replied.

"Are you nervous about wearing your glasses to school today?"

"Yes."

Mommy smiled. "It won't be so bad. Your

friends have seen other kids in glasses."

"They haven't seen me," I told her.

But when I got to school, it *wasn't* too bad. Nancy and Hannie and I were the first ones to reach our classroom. Even Ms. Colman wasn't there.

Nancy had already seen my glasses, so she didn't say anything about them. But Hannie said, "Oh, cool! Pink glasses!"

"Do you really like them?" I asked.

"I really do."

The other kids started to arrive. Some of them didn't even notice my glasses. Two of them just said, "Oh, Karen, you got glasses."

Then Ms. Colman came in.

"Why, Karen," she said. "I like your glasses very much."

"So do I," said Natalie Springer. Natalie Springer is in my class, too. She is the only other person who wears glasses. Hers have gold rims. Natalie has worn glasses since before kindergarten.

"Thank you," I said to Ms. Colman and Natalie. Then I added, "Guess what. I have

46

two pairs of glasses. I have blue ones for reading and these pink ones for the rest of the time."

"Gosh," said Natalie. She looked impressed.

But nobody else was paying much attention. Whew!

Then Ricky Torres came in. He saw me and my glasses right away.

"Ooh-ooh. Four-eyes!" he cried. "Hey, Karen. Are you just blind or are you as blind as an ugly old bat?"

"You are so dumb, Ricky," I said. "I am not blind at all. With my glasses on, I can see just fine. And besides, I think it's mean to tease about being blind. What if I really *were* blind?"

Ricky has hated me ever since the time I broke my wrist and he broke his ankle. We got casts at the same time. Each of us got lots of people to sign our casts. Ricky even got some baseball player to sign his. But *I* got a witch and an actress and Mr. Tastee to sign *my* cast. The witch was old Mrs.

Porter who lives next door to Daddy. The actress was a friend of Mommy's. And Mr. Tastee drives the Mr. Tastee ice-cream truck all over town. The kids in our class liked my autographs better than Ricky's.

Ricky has never forgiven me for that.

"Blind as a bat," Ricky said one more time, just to make me mad.

I looked at Ms. Colman. She was writing on the chalkboard. Her back was turned, so I stuck my tongue out at Ricky.

He did not stick his out at me, though. Instead he said, "School pictures are coming up, Miss Movie Star Brewer. Just think how *your* picture will look now."

I hadn't thought about that, but I didn't see what the big problem was.

"So I won't wear my glasses when the photographer takes my picture, Mr. Smarty-pants," I whispered loudly to Ricky. "You are so stupid. I can take my glasses off for a minute."

Ms. Colman clapped her hands. "Okay, class. Take your seats, please."

I stuck my tongue out at Ricky again. This time he stuck his out at me.

Then we sat down at our desks.

Teacher's Pet

All morning, Ricky called me Four-eyes and Bat-woman. He only whispered the names, so Ms. Colman wouldn't hear him.

All morning, I tried to ignore him.

That was not too hard.

First of all, we had art class. I just love art class. It is gigundo fun. Mr. Mackey comes into our room with his art cart, which is loaded with very wonderful supplies: paint and paper and crayons and glue and Magic Markers and scraps of things. Then he tells us what we are going to make.

"Today," he said, "we will make outer space pictures."

I wore my pink glasses while I listened to Mr. Mackey. I switched to my blue ones when I began my picture.

"Bat-woman!" whispered Ricky.

I pretended I didn't hear him. When I had finished my picture, I put my pink glasses back on.

Soon art class was over. Ms. Colman gave us two worksheets full of subtraction problems. I switched from my pink to my blue glasses.

"Four-eyes!" said Ricky.

I was getting a little bit mad. But Hannie nudged me. She passed me a note which I opened up in my lap. With my glasses on, I could read it perfectly. It said: *Yicky Ricky is picky and sticky.*

I tried not to giggle.

Then I worked very hard on my subtraction problems. And guess what — after

lunch, Ms. Colman gave our worksheets back. I got 100 percent on both of them. Two 100 percents!

"I'm very proud of you, Karen," said Ms. Colman.

In reading class, I followed all the directions on the board and I did all of my work perfectly. I had to switch my glasses a lot, so Ricky called me Four-eyes and Bat-woman about five times. But what did I care? I got 100 percents on everything!

At the end of the day, Ms. Colman called me to her desk. It was Free Reading time, and I was just starting a book about a bear named Paddington. I hated to put it down.

But I hated even more to hear what Ms. Colman said: "Karen, I am going to move you to the front row of the classroom."

"But why?" I cried. Had she seen Hannie pass me the note? Hannie and Nancy and I had tried so hard to be good. "I've been good." I told her. "At least, I have *tried* to be good."

That was the honest truth.

"Karen, this doesn't have anything to do with being good or bad," Ms. Colman told me. "It's because of your eyes. You'll see better up front. I've noticed how many times you had to switch your glasses today."

I nodded. That *had* been a pain.

"So please take your things out of your desk. You will be trading desks with Hank Reubens. He can move to your old seat. I'll talk to him while you clear out your desk."

I thought of saying that I did not want to

trade with Hank Reubens, but you don't argue with teachers. Even one as nice as Ms. Colman.

Of course everyone wanted to know what Hank and I were doing when they saw us taking the things out of our desks. Finally Ms. Colman said, "Karen is moving to the front row, boys and girls. She will be able to see the board better from there."

When Hank and I had traded places, I was sitting right in front of Ms. Colman's desk. I liked that. But I did not like leaving Hannie and Nancy behind. And I bet they did not like sitting next to Hank. Hank bites the erasers off of his pencils.

As if these things were not bad enough, Ricky thought of a new nickname for me. When school was over that day, he walked by me singing, *"Teacher's pet, teacher's pet. Karen is the teacher's pet."*

I will get you, Ricky Torres, I thought.

I put on my pink glasses and left the classroom.

Baby Karen

I thought about Ricky Torres all weekend.
How could I get back at him? He had called
me Four-eyes and Bat-woman and the teacher's pet. I already called him Yicky Ricky.
And I had called him Mr. Smarty-pants. But
those things did not seem bad enough.
Besides, it was not at all nice of him to tease
me just because I had to get glasses. Nobody
teased him when he got a cast on his ankle.

On Sunday afternoon, Nancy came over.
She found me in my room, sitting in my

rocking chair. Goosie was in my lap. I was wearing my pink glasses. Goosie was wearing the blue ones.

"What are you doing?" asked Nancy.

"Goosie and I are thinking of ways to get back at Yicky Ricky. He is so mean."

"And picky and sticky," added Nancy. (She had seen Hannie's note.)

Nancy and I laughed.

"What ideas have you thought of?" asked Nancy.

"None," I answered. "Not one single good one."

The next morning I could think of just one thing to do about Ricky and my glasses. I forgot to bring my glasses to school. Actually, I forgot them on purpose. I left both pairs of glasses on the bureau in my bedroom. Mrs. Dawes was driving Nancy and me to school, so Mommy did not see me run out of our house without my glasses.

I smiled all the way to school. If I didn't wear my glasses, then Ricky couldn't tease me, could he? He would look pretty silly calling me Four-eyes or Bat-woman when I didn't even have glasses on.

But the first thing Ms. Colman said when I walked into our classroom with Nancy was, "Karen, where are your glasses?"

"Huh?" I replied, as if I had just realized I wasn't wearing them.

"Are they in your book bag?" asked Ms. Colman. "You'd better put the pink ones on right now. You know you're supposed to wear them all the time."

I pretended to look through my book bag. "I — I guess I left them at home," I told Ms. Colman.

"Both pairs?"

I nodded.

"Karen," she said firmly, "you must remember them from now on."

"Okay," I replied. "Tomorrow I will wear them for sure."

I thought that was the end of that. Ricky came in and couldn't find anything to tease me about. I felt very happy. Until someone knocked on the door to our classroom during subtraction time.

In walked . . . Mommy! She called me over to the doorway.

"Ms. Colman phoned," she whispered. (I just knew everyone was watching Mommy and me. I was gigundo embarrassed.) "She said you forgot your glasses today. So here you go." She handed me both pairs. "And from now on, no more forgetting. You *must*

wear your glasses all the time. It's very important."

Mommy was forgetting to whisper. I know everyone heard her.

So I whispered, "Okay," and, "Thank you."

Then Mommy left.

In the cafeteria that day, Ricky came to the table Hannie and Nancy and I were sitting at.

"Ha-ha, Bat-woman," he said to me. "Now you *have* to wear your glasses when we have our pictures taken. Your mother said you must wear them all the time. If you don't, she'll be really upset . . . Baby Karen."

Oh, no. What a problem. Ricky was right. I *would* have to wear my glasses. And he had a new name for me. Baby Karen.

What was I going to do?

Mean Things to Do
to Ricky Torres

I was so mad that when I got home after school that day I went right to my room. I put on my blue glasses. I sat at my desk with a piece of paper in front of me. Across the top of it I wrote:

Mean Things to Do to Ricky Torres

Then I thought for awhile. Finally I wrote:

1. Tell him he smells.

That wasn't true, but so what. I was not as blind as a bat, either.

Then I wrote:

2. Put my strawberry eraser in his desk and tell Ms. Colman he stole it.

That was really mean, plus it would be lying. I would never do it. But I left it on the list anyway.

Next I wrote:

3. Tattle on him to Ms. Colman about the names he calls me.

4. Put a worm in his lunch box.
5. Put pepper (lots of it) in his lunch box.

I paused to think. I decided I needed ten mean things. So I added:

6. Hide his reading book.
7. Tell him his eyes have turned orange. Then have Nancy tell him his eyes have turned orange. Then have Hannie and maybe Natalie tell him his eyes have turned orange. Laugh at him if he checks them in a mirror.
8. Tell him that Mollie Foley from Mrs. Fulton's room says she's in love with him and wants to kiss him on the playground.
9. Ask him to see-saw with me during recess. When my end is on the ground, I'll roll off and say, "Ooh, my leg," like I'm hurt. He will crash to the ground.
10. Tell him I will never ever speak to him again. Ever.

* * *

The next day, I folded my list up eight times. I put it in my lunch box. I brought it to school. I felt very smug, even with my glasses on.

I was all set to get back at Ricky Torres. But Ricky was absent.

Ricky's Glasses

Okay. So Ricky had a cold or something. I was sure he would be in school the next day. Since I was so sure, I brought the list with me again.

I was right. Ricky *was* in school. And — and he was wearing . . . *glasses!*

At first I thought he was making fun of me. His glasses were pretty ugly. They were brown and squarish.

"Very funny, Ricky," I said, as he slumped down at his desk. "Okay, you can take them off now." I was about to add, "By the way, did you know that you smell?"

But Ricky looked like he was trying not to cry. So I closed my mouth. When I opened it again, all I said was, "What's wrong?"

"They're real," Ricky whispered. "The glasses. They're real. I had to get them, just like you. That's where I was yesterday. At the eye doctor's and everything. Only I just have one pair of glasses."

I hardly knew what to say. Ricky had called me Four-eyes and Bat-woman. I could call him a name now. If I wanted. Only I could see how bad he felt.

Plus a big group of kids was gathering around Ricky. Ricky looked like he wished he were anywhere but sitting at his desk, wearing glasses.

"Four-eyes!" said Hank Reubens.

"Bat-*man!*" cried Nancy gleefully.

"Square-eyes!" added Hannie.

My friends were getting back at Ricky for me. Fine. He could stay in the back of the room with his glasses, and I could stay in the front with my glasses, and we would not have to bother each other at all.

That was what I thought. But guess what Ms. Colman did as soon as she had taken attendance that morning.

She smiled at our class. Then she said, "Boys and girls, we have another new glasses-wearer, so we will have to switch some places again. Ricky, you need to sit up front with Karen and Natalie."

Ricky groaned.

I could have told him there was no point. A few minutes later, he was sitting *right next to me.* Jannie Gilbert had moved back to Ricky's old seat.

Ricky and I looked at each other. Ricky narrowed his eyes. Then he stuck his tongue out at me — just the tip, so that Ms. Colman wouldn't see.

I stuck the tip of my tongue out at him. Then I passed him a note. It read: LEAVE ME ALONE!

Ricky passed one back. His read: REMER-BER SKOOL PICSHERS. (Ricky is not a very good speller.)

I took Ricky's note, corrected it, gave him a D+, and passed it back to him.

Ricky stuck the tip of his tongue out at me again.

I did not pay one speck of attention.

Later, Ms. Colman handed back some spelling tests. I got another 100 percent. Ricky got a 55 percent. He had spelled almost half of the words wrong. So he threw a spitball at me. It was disgusting. I knocked

it on the floor. It rolled under Ms. Colman's desk, but she did not see it.

I raised my hand. "Ms. Colman?"

"Yes, Karen?"

"Ricky threw a spitball at me. It's under your desk."

Ricky looked like he wanted to kill me.

"One more spitball, Ricky," said Ms. Colman, "and you will miss recess."

Ricky waited until Ms. Colman was helping someone in the back of the room. Then he opened his mouth. I think he was going to call me a name. But he closed his mouth instead. No matter what name he called me, I could call him one back.

I made a decision. No matter how mad I was at Ricky, I would not make him feel worse about his glasses.

Just before lunch, I threw away my list of mean things to do to Ricky.

Ricky Is a Gir-irl!

During recess on most days, Hannie and Nancy and I play hopscotch. We are very good. Sometimes we can get all the way to the fourth square on one turn. And we never miss on the hopping part, only the stone-throwing part.

On the day Ricky first wore his glasses to school, we were having an especially good game. It was my turn. My playing had gotten a lot better since I started wearing glasses. I was about to throw to the fifth square when I heard:

"Aughh! Cut it out!"

It was Ricky, and he had made me miss.

I whirled around. "What did you have to scream like that for?" I shouted to him. "You made me — "

I stopped. I looked at Hannie and Nancy. They looked at me.

Ricky was in trouble.

The other boys in our class had crowded around him.

"Four-eyes!" cried Hank Reubens.

"Bat-man!" called someone else.

Then Bobby Gianelli, who is a big bully, made a grab for Ricky's glasses. He tried to snatch them right off his face. "Cut it *out!*" yelled Ricky again. He darted away from Bobby.

"Hey!" hooted Hank. "Guess what. Ricky is a gir-irl! Karen wears glasses, Natalie wears glasses, Ms. Colman wears glasses. Now Ricky's got 'em!"

"Yeah, he *is* a girl!" cried Bobby.

Bobby grabbed for Ricky's glasses again. That time, he almost got them.

70

I couldn't stand it any longer. I raced over to the boys.

"You stop that!" I yelled. "You leave Ricky alone! Don't touch his glasses, Bobby. Glasses are very, very expensive."

"*Yeah*," said Hannie and Nancy firmly. They were standing beside me.

Ricky looked miserable. I knew just how he felt. Or anyway, I knew almost how he felt. I sure was glad that nobody had made a ring around me on the playground and tried to take off my glasses.

"And Ricky is not a girl just because he wears glasses," I added.

Everyone had stopped yelling. They were staring at me. "My daddy wears glasses," I said, "and my stepdaddy wears glasses. . . . *So there.*"

Ricky was just staring at me. I couldn't tell what he was thinking.

Bobby backed away from Ricky. He looked sort of ashamed.

But Ricky yelled, "Shut up, Karen! Just shut up! I don't need help from a *girl*. Go

back to your dumb old hopscotch game."
Then he pushed his way through the circle
of kids. "I can stand up for myself, Karen!"
he cried. And he added, "Ugly-puss." He
ran away to the swings and sat by himself.

I stood where I was. I felt like I had been
stung.

A couple of the boys snickered at me, but
Hannie said, "Come on, Karen. Let's go
back to our game."

"Yeah," added Nancy. "You can take
your turn over. Ricky made you miss before.
That wasn't fair."

But all I could say was, "Ricky has a new
name for me. Ugly-puss."

"Call him Ugly-puss back," suggested
Hannie.

"No," I replied. "What's the point?"

Hannie and Nancy and I finished our
game. Nancy won.

"Are you having trouble seeing?" Nancy
asked me.

I shook my head. I could not say anything.

But it didn't matter. The bell rang. Recess was over.

Ricky and I did not speak to each other all afternoon. We did not stick the tips of our tongues out at each other. We did not even look at each other. I guess we were too embarrassed.

I could not wait to get home.

Ugly-puss

As soon as I got home that afternoon, I ran upstairs to my room. I did not stop for a snack. I did not stop even when Andrew said, "Hey, Karen, Mommy bought peanuts today."

I love peanuts, but peanuts would not make me feel better.

"No, thank you," I said to Andrew.

I closed the door to my room.

"Ugly-puss," I said out loud. Was I really ugly when I wore my glasses?

Then I thought a horrible thought. What

if I was ugly with*out* my glasses? What if I was just plain ugly? Maybe I was silly to think I could be a movie star.

Knock, knock, knock.

Someone was at my door.

"Go away, Andrew," I said. I still didn't want any peanuts.

But somebody who wasn't Andrew said, "It's not Andrew. It's me."

Nancy.

I did not really want to see Nancy, either. But I said, "Come in."

Nancy opened the door. Then she closed it behind her.

"Am I *really* ugly?" I asked Nancy.

"You? Ugly? Of course not."

"But Ricky called me an Ugly-puss."

"He was just mad because he has to wear glasses now, too."

I didn't say anything.

"Karen, you hardly look any different when you wear your glasses," said Nancy.

"I don't? Watch this." I was wearing my pink glasses. I put the blue ones on Goosie.

"There," I said. "See how different Goosie looks?"

"Goosie," said Nancy, "is a stuffed cat. No one expects cats to wear glasses. That's why he looks different."

"But maybe I really am ugly," I said to Nancy. "Even without glasses."

"Just because Ricky said so?" replied Nancy. "Do you believe everything Ricky says? If he told you you were a cow, would you believe him?"

77

I giggled. "No."

"Okay. Then forget what he said. I am your friend. And I am saying you look just fine, with your glasses on or with your glasses off."

"Like a movie star?" I asked.

Nancy shrugged. "I don't know. Some people in the movies wear glasses, some don't."

"That's true," I admitted. I felt better. "Want some peanuts, Nancy?"

"Sure," she replied, and we ran downstairs to find Andrew.

The next day, I did not want to wear my glasses in school. But I wore them anyway.

I did not want to sit next to Ricky, but I sat next to him anyway.

I didn't look at him. I didn't talk to him. I just did my work. And I got 100 percents everywhere. Switching my glasses helped a lot.

That day, Ricky called me a name every time I switched my glasses. That was seven times — five times in the morning, and two times in the afternoon.

On Friday, he didn't bother.

I felt like I wasn't even sitting next to him.

I had almost forgotten about glasses and movie-star smiles and Ricky. Then Ms. Colman said, "Boys and girls, remember that we will have our pictures taken on Monday. So get ready to look your best, and practice your smiles."

Oh, no. School pictures. Somehow, I had almost forgotten about them, too.

Next to me, Ricky began to snicker.

Ms. Colman heard him. "Mr. Torres?" she said. "Is there something funny that you'd like to share with the class?"

"No," answered Ricky. I peeked over at him just long enough to see that his face had turned red.

Good.

But what was I going to do about Monday? I would have to think very hard over the weekend.

Karen's Problem

That Friday wasn't just any Friday. It was a special Friday. It was a Going-to-Daddy's Friday.

I was excited and nervous. I was excited because Andrew and I are always excited about going to Daddy's. I was nervous because no one at the big house had seen me in my glasses yet. Not even David Michael. (He doesn't go to my school.)

Would David Michael tease me? He might, since sometimes he can be just like Ricky. Sam is a big tease, too. So I was nervous.

When Mommy let Andrew and me out of the car at Daddy's, she called, "Good-bye, Karen! Good-bye, Andrew! Have fun!"

"Good-bye, Mommy! We will!" we called back.

But I did not run to Daddy's front door as fast as usual.

Andrew did, though. He opened it and stepped inside.

I followed him. I did not call out, "We're here!" like I usually do.

So Andrew did it. "We're here," he said.

Even though his voice is not as loud as mine, everyone came running.

"Oh, Karen. Your glasses!" exclaimed Daddy. "I like them very much."

"You chose the perfect frames," said Elizabeth.

"I did?" I began to smile.

"You look distinguished," added Sam.

"Really?" I didn't know what "distinguished" meant and I was afraid to ask. Sometimes Sam teases me with big words.

But Charlie helped me out. He said, "Sam

means you look dignified and important. Like a professor or something. A *pretty* professor," Charlie added quickly. (Charlie doesn't like to hurt people's feelings.)

"Kristy?" I asked.

"You look like my Karen," she said.

That was just what I needed to hear.

The rest of the evening was fine, except for one little thing. When my big-house family sat down to dinner, David Michael began calling me Professor. I do not think he was being mean. I think he was trying to be nice. He had heard Charlie say I look like a professor. And he knows that Charlie is usually nice and doesn't tease.

But I did not want to look like a professor. I wanted to look like a movie star.

I decided to talk to Kristy.

Bedtime is usually a good talking time, so after we had finished our reading, I said, "Kristy?"

"Yes?" Kristy was plugging in the night-light that I got at Disney World.

"Monday is school-picture day," I told her.

"Oh, great! Do you know what you're going to wear?"

"Yes. I know about everything except my glasses. I can't decide whether to wear them. Ricky Torres says I'm an Ugly-puss."

"You are not an Ugly-puss," said Kristy. She sat down on the bed and put her arm around me.

"I think I look like a dork with my glasses on."

"Then don't wear them."

"Mommy gets mad when I don't wear them," I replied.

"She won't mind for just a minute."

"She might. Besides, Mommy never takes off her glasses when she has her picture taken. Neither does Natalie. Neither does Ms. Colman. I think," I said finally, "that I will feel like a dork if I leave them on, and I will feel like a wimp if I take them off. I do not know *what* to do."

Kristy gave me a butterfly kiss on my cheek. "I have an idea," she said. "I'll tell you about it tomorrow. Try to go to sleep now, okay?"

"Okay," I said. "Thank you, Kristy."

"You're welcome."

I fell asleep right away.

Spectacles

"Today," Kristy told me at breakfast on Saturday, "we are going to the library, Karen."

"And I will drive you there," Charlie added grandly.

"Why are we going to the library?" I asked. I like the library a lot, but Kristy and Charlie sounded quite mysterious.

"You'll see," was all Kristy would answer.

"Hey, Professor," said David Michael from across the table. "Will you return my library books for me?"

"Sure," I replied. I still could not decide whether I liked being called Professor.

Charlie dropped Kristy and me off at the library just as it was opening. Kristy led me into the children's room. We were the only people there, except for a librarian.

"May I help you?" she asked us.

"Thank you," said Kristy, "but we have to do this ourselves. I want to show my sister some pictures of people who wear glasses."

The librarian smiled. I frowned. What was Kristy up to?

Kristy took me by the hand. She walked me to a shelf labeled HOLIDAY BOOKS. She pulled out a bunch of Christmas stories.

"Notice anything?" she asked as we leafed through the books.

"Santa Claus wears glasses!" I exclaimed. "So does Mrs. Claus sometimes."

Then Kristy went to another shelf. She handed me a copy of *Winnie-the-Pooh*. I love that book.

"Take a look through it," said Kristy.

"Owl wears glasses!" I cried. Then I remembered that I was in a library and should keep my voice down.

Next, Kristy handed me a huge, fat book of stories with pictures by a man named Walt Disney. "Look!" I whispered loudly. "Geppetto wears glasses in *Pinocchio*, and the White Rabbit wears them in *Alice in Wonderland*, and John in *Peter Pan*, and even Scrooge McDuck. And Doc! He's my favorite

dwarf. Kristy, let's see if Jacob Two-Two wears glasses."

We checked, but he doesn't. I was disappointed — until Kristy helped me find a book called *Spectacles* about a pair of *magic* glasses.

"Boy," I said as we left the library with *Spectacles* under my arm. "An awful lot of important people wear glasses — even if most of them *are* boys!"

School-Picture Day

On Monday morning, I woke up in my bed at the little house. It was school-picture day. I still did not know whether I was going to wear my glasses. I *liked* my glasses okay. I just did not know whether to wear them.

"Karen?" said Mommy. She stuck her head in my door. "Are you awake?"

"Mmm," I replied. I was mostly awake.

"Don't forget what day this is."

"I already remembered."

Mommy laughed. "Do you want some

help choosing your clothes, or do you know what you're going to wear?"

"I think I will wear my dress that is blue on top and blue and black plaid on the bottom. I will wear a blue ribbon in my hair."

"Perfect," said Mommy. "That is a very good choice."

Mommy drove Nancy and me to school that morning. Nancy was ready for her

picture, too. She was wearing a red sweater over a white blouse. On the collar of the blouse were red flowers with green leaves. And tied on one side of her head was a huge red bow.

We were very excited.

The ride to school seemed to take forever. When Mommy finally pulled up in front of Stoneybrook Academy, she turned to look at me.

"Karen?" she asked. "Are you going to wear your glasses when the photographer takes your picture?"

I sighed. "I don't know, Mommy," I answered. "I really don't know."

"That's okay, sweetie," she said.

But she didn't say whether to wear them or not. I knew I would have to decide for myself. At least Mommy would not be mad if I took the glasses off for my picture. That just showed how much Ricky knew.

Nyah, nyah, nyah.

Now all I had to do was decide whether to be a dork or a wimp.

Nancy and I walked to our classroom. Every kid who came in looked very dressed up. Some of the boys were even wearing suits and ties.

I checked the glasses-wearers. Natalie's were on. So were Ricky's. But he might take them off later. My pink ones were on, of course.

When Ms. Colman came into the room, she clapped her hands.

"Please take your seats, boys and girls," she said.

We sat down. We stopped talking.

"The cameraman is here," announced Ms. Colman. "He is setting up his equipment in the gym. The kindergarteners and first-graders will have their pictures taken soon. Then it will be our turn. You will have your individual pictures taken first. Afterward, we will have our class picture taken."

Well, the little kids sure took their time. Our class waited and waited for them. What could possibly take so long?

But at last the school secretary called Ms. Colman on the intercom.

"Your class may go to the gym now," she said.

"Thank you," Ms. Colman replied. "Okay, class. Line up at the door — quietly."

We lined up, but I don't know how quiet we were. It's hard to be quiet when you are very, very excited.

I wiggled in between Hannie and Nancy. I noticed that Ricky was at the head of the line.

He is so pushy.

Our line filed out of our classroom and headed for the gym.

"Here we go!" I said to Hannie and Nancy.

CLICK!

When we reached the gym, the first-graders were still there. They were not finished yet. Boo.

"The secretary called us too early," I told Hannie and Nancy. "Now we will have to wait in line."

I do not like waiting in line.

But at last the first-graders left. The photographer turned to our class.

"Is everybody ready?" he asked.

"Yes!" we cried.

"Who's first?"

"Me! I'm first!" said Ricky. He was still at the head of the line.

The photographer led Ricky to a chair in front of a pale blue screen. He stood behind his big camera. "Smile!" he said to Ricky.

"Okay," Ricky replied. But before he smiled, he took off his glasses. He looked at me and stuck out his tongue. *Then* he looked at the photographer and smiled.

"What a wimp," I whispered to Hannie and Nancy. But I wasn't sure I meant it. If I took my glasses off, too, then I could give my best movie-star smile.

CLICK! The photographer took Ricky's picture.

Natalie was next. She sat in front of the blue screen.

"Smile!" said the photographer.

Natalie smiled. She was wearing her glasses.

I looked at Ms. Colman. I imagined her standing with our class when we had the group picture taken. Her glasses would be on. And suddenly I knew what I was going

96

to do. Only I had to get something out of my desk in our classroom first.

"Save my place!" I whispered loudly to Hannie.

"Where are you going?" she asked me.

"Can't tell. It's a secret."

I ran to Ms. Colman. I whispered my secret in her ear. Ms. Colman smiled. Then she gave me permission to go to our classroom. When I reached it, I took something out of my desk and ran back to the gym.

I got there just in time. Hannie was having her picture taken. My turn would come next.

When the photographer called to me, I walked proudly to the chair in front of the screen. I left my pink glasses on. Then I pulled the something out of the pocket of my dress — my blue glasses. They were fastened to a chain that the optometrist had given me. I had not used the chain before, but I needed it now. I slipped the chain over my head so that I was wearing the blue glasses like a necklace.

Now it was my turn to stick my tongue out at Ricky. Then I smiled at the photographer and his camera went CLICK! I had worn *both* pairs of glasses in *my* picture.

Ricky stared at me with his mouth open.

When all of my classmates had had their pictures taken, the photographer led us to some risers against the wall of the gym.

"Okay," he said, "taller kids in back, shorter kids in front."

When we were finally organized I was standing between Nancy and Yicky Ricky. Hannie was next to Nancy. Everyone was smiling.

And Ricky was wearing his glasses.

That afternoon on the playground I saw Ricky sitting on a swing by himself. I left Hannie and Nancy and ran over to him.

"Hey, Ricky," I said.

"Hey," he answered.

"Did you know," I began, "that Geppetto and the White Rabbit and Santa Claus all wear glasses?"

"Really?" replied Ricky. He sounded in-

99

terested. So I told him about Owl and Doc and John and Scrooge McDuck, too.

When I was finished, Ricky said, "I'm sorry I called you names."

I decided that maybe Yicky Ricky wasn't yicky after all.

Love, Karen

One week and four days later was a very special day. It was a Going-to-Daddy's Friday. It was also the day we got our school pictures back.

That was so much fun! I just love opening the envelope and seeing the pictures inside. There are two big, big ones. There are four medium-sized ones. There are sixteen tiny ones. The tiny ones are in rows on a sheet, and you have to cut them apart. And then there is the class picture, with everyone together.

I looked happily at the class picture. There I was, wearing both pairs of glasses. There was Ricky with his glasses and Ms. Colman with her glasses and Natalie with *her* glasses. It was the most wonderful picture I had ever seen.

"What do you think?" I asked Hannie and Nancy. They were examining their pictures, too.

"Great!" said Hannie.

"Neat!" said Nancy.

I think Mommy was surprised when she looked at the pictures and saw that I was wearing two pairs of glasses. But then she said, "I am proud of you, Karen." So I still felt happy.

Mommy kept one big picture and two medium pictures for her and Seth. The other big picture and medium pictures were for Daddy and Elizabeth. All the little ones were for me. So was the class picture.

When Andrew and I got to Daddy's that night, I was so, so, so excited.

"Here are my pictures! Here are my pictures!'' I cried, before I had even taken my jacket off.

''Pretty nice, Professor,'' said David Michael.

''Beautiful, '' said Daddy and Elizabeth.

''They look just like my Karen,'' said Kristy.

After dinner, I took the little pictures up to my bedroom. I found a pair of scissors and sat down at my table. Then I put on

my blue glasses. Very carefully, I cut the pictures apart.

"There," I said to Moosie. "Now I have to sign them."

I wrote "Love, Karen" on the back of every picture.

Here are the people the pictures were for: Mommy, Daddy, Seth, Elizabeth (for their wallets), Nannie, Kristy, Charlie, Sam, David Michael, Andrew, Emily, Hannie, Nancy, Natalie, my friend Amanda Delaney, and Ricky Torres.

I knew just how I would give people my pictures, too. I would hold each one out and say, "Here. This is for you from me."

Except for Ricky's picture. I would hide Ricky's picture in his desk and let him find it by himself.

I sighed. That was a good idea. Then I took off my blue glasses. I put on the pink ones. I ran downstairs. It was time to start handing out my school pictures.

L. GODWIN

About the Author

ANN M. MARTIN lives in New York City and loves animals, especially cats. She has three cats of her own, Gussie, Woody, and Willy, and one dog, Sadie.

Other books by Ann M. Martin that you might enjoy are *Stage Fright, Me and Katie (the Pest)*, and the books in *The Baby-sitters Club* series.

Ann likes ice cream and *I Love Lucy*. And she has her own little sister, whose name is Jane.